Tom Hellberg is a retired architectural draughtsman who has also worked as an advertising manager at Caduceus Journal. He has been involved in highlighting the need for action on climate change with both the Green Party, Friends of the Earth and UKWIN.

I would particularly like to thank my brother and sister over the many years it has taken to put this down on paper, and their continuing support for this project.

Tom Hellberg

CLIMATE COUNTDOWN

T.C Henry

AUSTIN MACAULEY PUBLISHERS™

LONDON • CAMBRIDGE • NEW YORK • SHARJAH

ISBN 9781398453982 (Paperback)
ISBN 9781398453999 (ePub e-book)

www.austinmacauley.com

First Published 2022
Austin Macauley Publishers Ltd®
1 Canada Square
Canary Wharf
London
E14 5AA

This is a long list but I would particularly mention Janet Alty and Chris Philpott for their advice on earlier drafts. Gitta Ashworth for letting me use her Apple Mac. Special thanks to James Flowerdew who has kept me up to date with website design. To Raga Woods, Clare Saunders and Chris Keene, friendship cemented on the campsite.

Chapter 1

Introduction

The forerunner of the *Extinction Rebellion* and the *UK student climate network* movements, the Climate Camp relied on land squats at key targets around England and Scotland from 2006 to 2010. Climate change is now on the top of the agenda and surely will never go away again (like the current pandemic).

'If you go to one demonstration and then go home, that's something, but the people in power can live with that. What they can't live with is sustained pressure that keeps building, organisations that keep doing things, people that keep learning lessons from last time and doing it better the next time.'

The UK Climate Camp movement—*(CCA),* which started in 2006—was a pioneering grassroots environmental movement set up for action on site. Their annual camp was to confront the bonds of order and fear which hold capitalism together. George Monbiot called the camp 'better organised, more democratic and more disciplined than any (protest) I have seen.' '…running water, sanitation, hot food twice a day, banks of computers.' 'I place my hope in ordinary people, who, throughout history, have shown an incredible ability, even in brief flashes, to resist, to join together, and occasionally to win.'

2006 saw an unprecedented, global attack on Climate Science. Vested fossil-fuel burning interests had successfully blocked governmental action all over the rapidly warming world. Ironically, the *Camp for Climate Action* was already deeply infiltrated from the start by undercover police, albeit resigned to state interference.

It is widely believed that 300000 people each year are already needlessly dying as a direct result of climate change, according to the *World Health Organisation.* 'Faced with the full facts about climate change and the massive reduction in emissions necessary over a very short period of time, it's all too easy to either deny the problem or conclude that it's too late, that it's an issue so large and entrenched that it's without a solution. We found it remarkable that scientists' predictions of global catastrophe under business-as-usual had hardly animated radicals. We wanted to move away from denial. We wanted to say that the future is, literally, in our hands,' wrote Paul Sumburn. An EU poll known as the 'Eurobarometer' poll showed around 60% were concerned about the environment at that time (probably more now).

Between 1961 and 2010, it has been estimated that global warming depressed the per capita wealth in the poorest nations by between 17% and 30%.

It was January 2006, a meeting had been convened via email. I can't even recall who had sent it to me. There were perhaps just a mere 50 people attending on that day at *MERCi*: the Manchester Environmental Resource Centre. This was a converted canal warehouse in Ancoats (Bridge 5 Mill). It was to be my first experience of a world in which ideas, rather than products, were to be the ruling theme. I admit to being overwhelmed by the ambitions of this fledgling group – nothing in my life had prepared me for such an experience. It was as if the campers bought into the idea that they were on a shared experiment; convinced they were reacting to ecological breakdown before everybody else.

In 53 years, nothing had suggested such an unusual opportunity could arise. In the next few years, it permanently changed my outlook on life. The beauty of the Camp was that it offered a glimpse of communal living and it gave us an insight into what capitalism is and what it is doing to our lives. Crucially, for anti-capitalist environmentalism, the flat hierarchy of the Camp stood as opposed to the obverse of capitalism.

In the real world, these decisions are made by a tiny minority of people...and the decisions are made in accordance with the profit motive. Both human beings and natural resources are exploited, degraded and despoiled to this end. The camps were organised the other way around: bottom-up.

Paulo Freire wrote: '...My consciousness is occupied with all sorts of myths in relation to my situation. This conformity is being fed by oppressive influences which feed my consciousness continuously – myths like the myth of equal opportunities in education, the myth of private property as a necessary basis for personal success, the myth that white people are superior to other races, the myth that women are more emotional and therefore less strong than men.' The campers were to break out of that box.

I had to take on trust with many new faces. Their basic premise was that Social Change and Climate Change could be addressed together 'by small, local groups doing action, education, training and political engagement at the grassroots level…' Even more startling was the fact that only six months later, this annual weeklong event would become an international template copied all over the world – the 'Climate Camp'.

I too bitterly remembered being among two million anti-war protesters tramping the streets of London, a legacy war of the attrition of Tony Blair, the horrors inflicted on the Third world in the name of neo-liberalism, of globalisation; I remember the first time I felt betrayed by those in whom I had once liked to place my trust. All I had left was an empty husk of nostalgia and dreams. Those lies cover up brutal acts of economic necessity, when in the 'National Interest.' Also '…our state's ability to guarantee its citizens' wellbeing is questionable.'

We have known the inevitable cost of having an unliveable planet but kicked the can down the road. In practice, this amounts to saying there cannot and must not be any tolerance for dissent. I had been quite active in the Green Party and a co-ordinator for FoE and had for a number of years edited the Green Party regional newsletter for the Midlands.

'The grassroots community can become the intermediate micro-social space between the private and the public, macro-social spaces. It can protect individuals from becoming isolated, lonely, and withdrawn. At the mercy of the market – the language of *sustainable development* has entered mainstream politics and environmentalists aspired to be a leading force in shaping international agreements.'

'Our society institutes scarcity and deprivation, by framing life as a desperate rush for limited material wealth and status.' It can, contra-wise, open up the private sphere onto a space of common sovereignty, shielded from commodity relations, where individuals together determine for themselves their common needs and decide the most appropriate actions for satisfying them. It is at this level that individuals can (once again) become masters of their own destinies, their own way of life...' In the age of coronavirus, we fully understand this.

The previous camps I had been to before (as a teenager) were the holiday camp model, dedicated to leisure or entertainment, nothing serious—usually with a group now known as Plus, it had run Easter and Autumn camps—in Caister holiday camp and Trentham Gardens. It was with this group that I organised my first charity gig.

It was always anticipated, or so I was told, there would likely be informer(s)—but apart from the site appraisal group, which we were told was always kept closed—everything else was left wide open 'see if we care'. We were correct: there were at least two undercover police officers at most meetings. What was surprising, therefore, was how the sites came to be established at all.

I approached this new venture with the open mind it required. I was aware of how little snow we had in winter compared to my childhood; I had observed the accelerating pace of climate change over my lifetime. At that time, I was working as the advertising manager of a holistic magazine. My mother had been paralysed by a stroke and I was a part-time carer. It was escapism pure and simple.

What I was yet to learn was how hard it is to pull off living in a temporary, self-managed community for longer than a week. Unlike many utopian experiments, it was not on some remote hillside invisible to the world, but in the public gaze, fronting the world's media. Friendships would form quite easily. The life and well-being of the camp were based on mutual appreciation. *We no longer related to each other via the commodities we bought and sold in the marketplace, the cash in our pockets and the sale of our capacity to work.* We related directly as human beings, reliant on each other for our sustenance. I didn't believe that the vast majority of people would make that choice – and even so, I'm not prepared to see them forced to do so by some authoritarian government.

This had been foreseen to some extent by the United Nations with Agenda 21, the Rio summit of the initiative dating back to 1992. This had envisaged small local groups doing action, education, training and political engagement at the grassroots level...In practice, it became like being an Okie in California as of John Steinbeck's 'Grapes of Wrath.'

It seemed to be a natural, efficient way of organising the camp. Each person would have a task unique to them that is their personal interest and is the focus of their own individual attention. My interests were at the educational and zero-carbon end rather than direct-action, so I opted to run a workshop instead. I was one of around two hundred speakers at the first of these camps. After five annual Climate Camps in the UK (see Appendix 1), which were originally intended to be a one-off, have run their course. The camp model was copied overseas after this time. From the government standpoint, policing of the camps was greatly assisted by inside information from undercover police informants, and their intention, as published under the camp website. The enforcers of the status quo will always be the police.

Globalisation was a shared concern. Many veterans at the camp were pioneers of previous actions, like Newbury bypass and *Reclaim the Streets*, very active in the nineties. These were what the police would term 'domestic extremists' and many may have been machine wreckers.

Following the debate, the four key themes of the camp were to be: *education, direct action, sustainable living, and building a movement to effectively tackle climate change* – to develop sustainable solutions and challenge and pick a target. We were told the previous organisers had dropped out – but that was simply not true. This mass movement had started up; well before the Arab spring, at the G8 summit the previous year.

Education during the camp was to be seen as a process of learning and sharing knowledge located in particular ways of life. The ethos was designed to be self-correcting and an organic response to the climate crisis; looking for positive solutions – indicative of the huge increase in concern over the last two generations.

According to academics, the educational element at the camp was 'a site of open debate in which the best peer review argument should win'. Another important feature was non-violent direct action. It offered a realistic opportunity to challenge violence. Non-violent direct action has in the post-1945 era acquired an extraordinary pedigree arising from numerous campaigns worldwide. This issue will be discussed in Chapter 8.

Many of the niches previously available in the 1980s were not available to those fighting for social change (like living on the dole or squatting) are no longer feasible, thanks to an increasingly…punitive system. According to Mikheil Goldman, mass anxiety has somehow become a common experience, as is the onus is on *individual failure*. From the bedroom tax and imposition of workfare to the constant questioning of the disabled and single parents, changes to the welfare system have hit many hard. Meanwhile, the effects of austerity, from women's refuges to mental health services, have meant that those already suffering are made to suffer all over again. This *entirely intentional* grinding down of the majority of the population is in order to maintain the dominance of the establishment, rich and powerful. In this environment, the ability to take part in broader struggles can either be seen as an unaffordable luxury; or could present some novel ideas for resistance. Whether coronavirus will now bring this to resolution remains to be seen, but it has no respect for any one group, though it seems to be targeting the elderly.

Of course, there had been previous peace camps – such as Greenham Common, and the Faslane nuclear submarine base. I will compare these with the Climate Camp in the next chapter. 'We all know that as individuals and as societies we must make wrenching changes to avert increasingly large-scale disasters through climate change…it is an excellent initiative.'—wrote Milan Rai.

Chapter 2

The Historical Precedent

The 1990s saw widespread (and destructive) street protests in the UK. In December 1991, Twyford Down became the site of the UK's first road protest camp – *Dongas and Earth First!* United to hinder work on the new motorway. This cut through chalk down-land up on the main lorry route up from the port of Southampton. The machinery was sabotaged. It delayed work by a year. In response, in late 1994, the *Criminal Justice and Public Order Act,* came into force. The Bill was intended by Michael Howard to cripple civil protest and criminalise raves. He was home secretary in John Major's Conservative government. It introduced the concept of 'aggravated trespass', under the terms of which any 'additional conduct' while trespassing could constitute a crime.

Road protesters had not been good ambassadors for protest as they favoured sabotage of expensive earth-moving machinery. The state views violence in the hands of individuals as a danger undermining the legal system; as a danger of nullifying the legal process. The type of protest that was to follow later can be described as NVDA (Nonviolent Direct Action). Some activists see a nonviolent philosophy as absolutely essential at all times and only 'want the right to protest'. There are two types of direct action – against people and against property; NVDA should be the latter. Climate campers saw NVDA as only a tactic like 'locking on', a form of obstruction.

The State can rely on coercion; it has a huge arsenal of resources to draw on. It will be quick to confront any citizen behaviour seen as threatening 'actions resulting in damage to property'; and saboteurs, of course, fall into this category. Any element of *economic damage* automatically becomes a criminal offence. The media will follow this line. It is important to expect this sort of thing and be ready to deal with it. In 1985, the miners' strike and the Battle of the bean-field took place, the latter saw over 500 arrests in an attempt to enforce a high court ban on the 1985s Stonehenge free festival. The individual counts for nothing against the state and it won't let you forget it. Productive discussion at our first meeting planned to avoid violence; the campaign was to cope well with these issues – issues that have been faced throughout history.

What the government hadn't counted on was how this common threat would unify the very groups it was intended to divide. That was what the *Criminal Justice and Public Order Act* achieved. Instead of feeling marginalised, the cause of anti-road activists became synonymous with that of travellers, squatters and hunt saboteurs. In particular, the politicised eighties rave scene became the communal social focus for many people. After losing the M11 campaign and the blockade of Claremont Street in 1995, *Reclaim the Streets* (RTS) organised *Street Parties I and II* during that summer of 1995. Anger about road building was then at its zenith.

Other actions targeted the likes of Shell, the Nigerian Embassy and the Motor Show, in conjunction with *Rising Tide*.

I was angry about the extensive road-building program at the expense of public transport. For my part, I painted a banner which was draped on a bridge over the M6 near the National Exhibition Centre. This followed shortly after the approval of the Birmingham Northern Relief Road (a toll road), and the eviction of a protest camp on the proposed line of that motorway, near Coleshill.

Summer 1996 saw the massively popular M41 Street Party take place. It came out of the free party scene. Some 8,000 people occupied the M41 motorway in West London for nine hours of partying. Trees rescued from the construction path of the M11 were even planted in the carriageway.

'Direct action actually enables people to develop a new sense of self-confidence and an awareness of their individual and collective power. (It) is founded on the idea that people can develop the ability for *self-rule only through practice*, and proposes that *all persons directly decide the important issues facing them*. Direct action is seen not to be: just a tactic; it is individuals asserting their ability to control their own lives and to participate in social life without the need for mediation or control by bureaucrats or professional politicians. Direct action encompasses a whole range of activities, from organising co-ops to engaging in resistance to authority. (It) places moral commitment above positive law.'

The Metropolitan policeman Jim Boyling had infiltrated RTS. He was among those charged alongside fellow road activists for Public Order offences. In 1997, he gave evidence under oath in court using his alias Jim Sutton – the identity he had assumed for his undercover work. He was now committing perjury. Boyling was acquitted along with other protesters, but one activist, John Jordan, was convicted of assaulting a police officer. Boyling had established himself as a trusted member of the campaign group; relied upon to turn up to both protests and weekly meetings. 'He was totally deeply embedded in the whole social network as well. Meetings often happened in the top room of a pub so he would be there and end up living with people,' said one activist.

Boyling was described as reticent and 'a nice bloke', a fitness fanatic with an asset unusual among the environmental campaigners: a van. He used it to transport equipment for demonstrations from, for instance, activists' homes. In reality, he was legend building, a role agreed and paid for by our government with a budget.

Over the last decade, a global movement has emerged which has called itself 'anti-capitalist'. This emergence has been a process of diverse movements making real links with one another: discussing, learning, reflecting and acting together.

The roots of passive resistance and consensus decision-making, however, go a lot further back than 'Reclaim the Streets'. Pointing to the importance of spatial organisation in protest, David Graeber describes a parallel strategy pursued by the Roman plebeians: '…the secession of the plebs, when commoners of the city abandoned their fields and workshops, camped outside the city and threatened mass defection.' Perhaps the earliest protest camp?

Influence 1: **The Levellers**

The social and historical context of the Levellers (or Diggers) was the collapse of the feudal system. The dissenter was '…every human being who resigns momentarily from the herd and thinks for himself.' The Enclosure Acts, and the preceding Black Death, had dispossessed a large number of peasants. The great fear among landed gentry was a possible revolt against enclosures. Misdemeanours such as hunting and trespassing were made offences punishable by death. The leading light was Gerald Winstanley. As the leader of the Diggers, he believed that it did not make any difference whether one lived under the enemy or under one's brother if one worked for a wage (he believed you were not free).

Levellers Day is still commemorated every year on 17 May. This marks the execution of three levellers on the orders of Thomas Cromwell on that day in 1649.

Influence 2: **The Quakers**

Quaker beliefs were '…heirs to an older radical tradition of dissent…that had been forged in the Civil War.' What made Quakers so troublesome to the establishment in their day was their refusal to accept authority. Their reaction against religious intolerance bred a sense of kinship. They were perhaps the first to grasp that industrial civilisation is, in fact, more vulnerable than empires based on religious power. They also lived through a time of momentous change, with first the Enclosure Acts and then Industrial Revolution.

'It is the Christian's right and duty to fight evil on all levels of society, power and authority, including in the heavenly and ecclesiastical realm.'

During the run-up to the Industrial Revolution, it would be the Luddites, many who espoused the Quaker faith, who would be the machine wreckers.

Influence 3: **The Committee of One Hundred**

Back in the UK, the *Campaign for Nuclear Disarmament* had, in 1958, adopted direct action as a possible method of campaigning against nuclear weapons. However, CND leadership was split over unlawful protest, largely because of disagreement about this tactic between the chair, Canon John Collins and Russell. At that time, a mass demonstration was illegal under the *Public Order Act* (now repealed). The *Committee of 100* was split off as a separate organisation, because of that.

The Committee's main campaign tactic was the sit-down demonstration. It was not to be undertaken without at least two thousand volunteers pledging to take part. Demonstrators were recommended to remain limp if arrested and to refuse to co-operate in any way until inside the police station. '…We ask you to come *only if you are willing to accept this non-violent discipline.*'

Their first act of civil disobedience was outside the Ministry of Defence in Whitehall, London, on 18 February 1961. It was timed to coincide with the expected arrival of the American warship the USS Proteus on the River Clyde. Between 1,000 and 6,000 people took part. Somewhat to the surprise of the Committee, there were no arrests. However, that was to change – at the second sit-down demonstration on 29 April (Parliament Square), where there were all 826 arrests. This highlights the need to vary tactics as the state reacts to dissent.

That internal power struggle weakened the overall anti-nuclear campaign generally. CND was revived with the women's camp at Greenham Common, the proposed cruise missile site, and Faslane, the nuclear submarine base on Holy Loch in Scotland (see influence 5).

Influence 4: **The Zapatistas**

The Mexican *Zapatista* group takes its name from Emiliano Zapata, an agrarian reformer and commander, and in 1910, of the 'Liberation Army' of the South during the Mexican Revolution. In common with the *Diggers* in England, the issue was the lack of communal land rights. The Zapatistas timed their uprising to coincide with the implementation of NAFTA in 1994. The North American Free Trade Agreement, between Canada, US and Mexico. They were, however, crushed by the army and only then adopted Non-Violent Direct Action from that point on.

NAFTA led to a glut of cheap corn from US in Mexico. Farmers found the market for their domestic produce collapsed, but curiously the prices in the shops rose, instead of falling. Large tracts of the countryside now grow GM maize, mainly exported for animal feed. This directly led to the Peoples' Global Action (*PGA*) Network, globally coordinated days of action, the 'encounters' (encuentros), and summit mobilisations. The fledgling *Indymedia* website contributed to the creation of worldwide groups on the net; organisations and individuals, independent of the 'old left' institutions, parties, and unions.

The affinity group or 'Piquette' originates in Spain, as Bookchin asserts. Spanish 'grupo de afinidad', an organisation devised in pre-Franco days as the basis of the redoubtable, *Federación Anarquista Ibérica,* (Iberian Anarchist Federation). A group of people block a road or street with the purpose of demonstrating and calling attention to a particular demand. This is termed a 'piquetero' whose primary, *modus operandi,* is based on the Piquette. Social centres in towns and cities across Europe, self-managed factories in Argentina, seed sharing, small action collectives, prisoner support initiatives and independent publishing projects across the globe, are all modern examples.

Influence 5: **Faslane 365**

More than 1,100 anti-nuclear protesters had been arrested in just one year (2007), during a yearlong series of blockades and demonstrations at the UK's main submarine base in Scotland. There has been a camp outside the base for many years. There has also been sporadic action at the NSA/NRO Men with Hill US monitoring station.

Influence 6: **The Indian Independence movement**

Perhaps the most successful pioneer of NVDA was Gandhi, as part of the Indian independence movement. This preceded the partition of the country. During the *Dharasana Satyagraha*, a protest relating to salt taxes, two Indian women, Sarojini Naidu and Maulana Abul Kalam Azad, led marchers to a beating-up. 320 were injured. Publicity arising from this action was critical in bringing worldwide attention to the Gandhi movement.

I believe the Climate Camp model was learning by doing, not copycat rote learning. Occupying space was the preferred method of choice for the Climate Camp, (as it was to be for the *Occupy* movement).

In different times and places, the same tactics have been adopted time and again, as described in this chapter. Some may be unfamiliar; I was certainly not influenced by them, but they were mentioned by some. Each of us (was) trying, in our different ways, to return a sense of humanity to our existence. We were destined to find out all over again by learning the hard way, as I shall describe. Now we have social media; 'these things are everywhere'.

Chapter 3

The Failure to Deal with the Climate Crisis

The theory behind the greenhouse effect had its origins in the nineteenth century with the theories of Nobel Prize-winning Swedish physicist Svante Arrhenius. In 1896, Arrhenius calculated the potential warming impacts of rising CO^2 on the earth's surface temperature. Arrhenius's book, *Worlds in the Making,* laid out what he termed the 'hot-house' theory of the earth's atmosphere. This is that the atmosphere maintains a 'saturated' greenhouse effect, controlled by water vapour content and $CO^{2.}$ This came to be known as the *general circulation model*.

He had picked up on the work of Irish physicist John Tyndall who, in 1861, posited that human-generated gases (such as carbon dioxide and ethylene) could transmit enormous volumes of heat. French physicist Joseph Fourier had previously observed that our world should have been much colder than it was in reality, given the earth's distance from the sun. He concluded that the planet's atmosphere had the ability to trap great volumes of heat (in a similar manner to a human greenhouse). So Fourier may actually have been the first to understand what is now termed the 'greenhouse effect'.

By 1958, it was revealed that this effect had been increasing year on year for decades. Sir Charles Kelling published his results; then another physicist, Sir James Lovelock, introduced the parallel concept of *Gaia*. This was the concept of the earth as a single, complex, dynamic system; it seized the popular imagination. It was further reinforced in the public mind by pictures of the earth taken by the astronaut Richard Armstrong. 'Gaia' is the personification of the Earth as a Greek deity. In religious terms, this belief is Noetics. The Intergovernmental Panel on Climate Change (IPCC) was established by the World Meteorological Organisation and United Nations Environmental Programme (UNEP) in 1988 to assess scientific, technical, and socioeconomic information that was relevant in understanding *human-induced* climate change, and its potential impacts. It promoted what is generically termed, the *general-circulation model,* as previously described. It continues to promote and research in this subject area.

According to the IPCC '97%' model, failing to cut CO^2 emissions now by 6% per annum will mean that by 2022, we would need to cut by 15% per annum, a next to impossible task. When the first camp was staged, the level was 400ppm; by 2020 it had increased by another 15ppm. Global emissions of carbon dioxide ($CO2$) have increased by almost 50 percent since 1990. Not in the right direction.

There are no shortcuts to the technological, economic, political and cultural changes needed to tackle climate change. That was true 30 years ago when the IPCC was formed. The only thing that has changed is the time in which we have left to do anything.

The required policies include rapid and deep de-carbonisation of the energy sector, end-use electrification including of most vehicles, heating and industrial processes, improving the energy efficiency of buildings, appliances, and industry, and managing land-used to reduce carbon and methane emissions.

Petroleum lobby groups were orchestrating another agenda: fake news, to debunk this assertion. Alternative explanations, such as the 'electric sun' model, were promoted to posit that variation in output over geological time was significant, the result of variations in the Earth's position in relation to the Sun. In this scenario, ground currents are said to be induced in response to surges in solar auroras. Auroras at the poles vary with the intensity of the sunspots.

These auroras are caused by the interaction of plasma with the earth's magnetic field, streams of charged particles from the sun; which astrophysicists term the *solar wind*. So variations in sunspots could have a slight climatic effect. According to Milankovitch, cool summers and relatively mild winters over a geological time scale could be sufficient to trigger the development of glacial periods, in combination with small variations in the Earth's distance from the Sun. How significant is this? According to NASA, solar activity has dropped to the lowest level in 200 years. The maximum of this next cycle—measured in terms of sunspot number, a standard measure of solar activity level—could be 30 to 50% lower than the most recent one.

The sun is going through a stage known as a solar or Maunder Minimum. This is where the solar activity that ignites solar flares or sunspots has decreased. It's a normal cycle and one that has been linked to the mini ice age that lasted more than 50 years, starting in the mid-1600s. According to space weather since 2015, the number of days without a sunspot has been rising year after year. NOAA, NASA and others all appear to agree the sun is entering a solar minimum phase.

Professor of Mathematics Valentina Zharkova of Northumbria University, one of the first people to raise awareness of the decrease in solar activity, for a *Conversation That Matters* about the sun, its reduced activity and her reading of the impact it will have on temperatures on earth. The results show that the next cycle may be starting and could potentially spawn another 'Little Ice Age' a 'mini' ice age. Critics of the *general-circulation model* have latched on to this, dismissing the declared '97% consensus' as another example of 'confirmation bias'.

This makes us blind to data that disagrees with our beliefs, making us overly attentive to messages that agree with them. In 2011, psychologists suggested that the less we know about some complex issue, the more we resist trying to find out about it. It influences (among other things) visual attention to the news that climate change is serious.

'Optimism bias' is also very powerful – we know of various brain mechanisms that can ensure that a positive mood persists; a reduced level of neural coding of more negative than anticipated information (in comparison with more positive than anticipated information) in a critical region of the prefrontal cortex involved in decision-making. This means that we tend to downplay bad news and, even if we don't, we might not process it.

The extent of human influence is not all encompassing. Those scientists who branded the *general-circulation* model as 'unfit for...purpose' did agree on one thing. Global warming, for them, had become a pseudo-religion; dependent, they said, more upon dogma, rather than verifiable scientific truth. These reservations came from within a small group of researchers working within the Climate Research Unit (CRU) of the University of East Anglia, members of the IPCC. Internal emails from 2009 revealed that '...many of the uncertainties surrounding the cause of climate change will never be resolved because the necessary data are lacking.' Some IPCC members certainly saw it as being about redistributing wealth. It was more about *economics* than climate.

'First of all, developed countries have basically expropriated the atmosphere of the world community,' continued Edenhofer. Thus, in his opinion, coal and oil developers should pay *reparations* in the form of global carbon emission rights and taxes. Investor group, *Business Daily,* commented, 'UN War-mongers are seeking to impose a global climate reparations tax on everything from airline flights and international shipping, to fuel and financial transactions.'

'The Cancun agreement set up a "Green Climate Fund" to administer assistance to "poor" nations suffering from floods and drought due to global warming. The European Union, Japan and the United States...pledged $100 billion per year for poor nations, plus $30 billion in immediate assistance.'

Politically, it had taken interminable discussions to drag the environment up from the bottom of the agenda, like watching a lobster in a slowly boiling cauldron. Political leadership was no match for concerted fossil fuel lobbies. The automotive and fossil fuel industry in the US had set up the Global Climate Coalition back in 1989 to argue against rapid action and to cast doubt on the evidence. An analysis by Barry Saxifrage of Canada's *National Observer* shows that half the fossil fuels ever used by humans have been burned since 1990. The free market had failed to establish a price for carbon that would incentivise its reduction. Carbon rationing is one of the possible responses, a punitive tax on excessive carbon emissions. The UK landfill tax has been very successful in reducing landfills, by way of an example.

The half-hearted nature of COP talks compared to the previous success of an international ban on chlorofluorocarbons (CFC) refrigerants a few decades before is salutary. The Montreal Protocol, finalised in 1987, was the global agreement to protect the stratospheric ozone layer by phasing out the production and consumption of ozone-depleting substances (ODS).

The guiding principle for carbon offsetting is that, as far as the biosphere is concerned, a tonne of carbon here has exactly the same effect as a tonne of carbon anywhere else. So if it's cheaper to reduce emissions in India than it is in the UK, then achieve the same climate benefit in a more cost-effective manner by making the reduction in India. Inevitably, this concept creates an illusion that high-carbon activities enjoyed by wealthier individuals can continue by transferring the burden of action and sacrifice to others. Offsetting is not a given; for example, in planting trees to offset a flight, the trees will be long gone before the carbon in the jetstream is absorbed.

Processes on land are apparently responsible for taking up about a third of human CO_2 emissions. So for every kilo of carbon emitted by a car or a power plant, about 350 grams will end up in a tree trunk, a leaf, or decomposed into the soil. There is no consensus about exactly what is responsible for the growing strength of the land sink, but most likely it is a combination of more CO_2 in the atmosphere and nitrogen-containing chemicals from agriculture and industry.

Carbon offsetting for woodlands could offer a potential income for farmers who want to convert some (or all) of their land from sheep pasture to woodland. This would be funded by people and organisations who want to offset their emissions by buying carbon credits. For example, an individual may pay for carbon credits to compensate for their contribution to aviation emissions, or a business may buy carbon credits in order to meet corporate responsibility objectives. Finance is being leveraged on enormous scales to reforest landscapes in less developed countries. It's about time western countries dropped the double standards and took the same approach at home.

This would become a market-led initiative. In 2010, Carbon Trading globally amounted to $144bn. The floor price for carbon, as trade, continues to be too low to make any change economically. It also seems that many countries, like the USA, bought up large numbers of trades to *evade responsibility* for their domestic emissions.

The EU carbon-trading scheme (*ETS*) though, has (in parallel with the EU Biofuels directive) been a failure since its inception. Its aim was to police the energy market. The cap on emission will fall by 2.2% a year—the so-called linear reduction factor—until at least 2024. Whether this will put it back on track is open to question. Starting in 2005, it has seen the centre of frauds, such as to permit theft, recycling of carbon credits, and hacking of carbon accounts. The 2008 banking crisis did not help. Six were jailed in Germany for 'carousel trading' in which they imported emission permits without paying VAT and then sold them to each other, adding tax to the price and pocketing the difference. The scheme continues.

At that time, it was not the view of the UK government. '...If the environment was any further down its list of priorities at that time, it would have fallen off the bottom.' Jonathon Porritt had this to say: '...Any thought on the part of our NGO that "working the corridors of power" is still the best way of defending the environment is folly.' Some UK politicians had been openly hostile to ecology; Owen Patterson, for example, a former minister of agriculture, derided the 'green blob'. Bemoaning is unlikely to win allies.

David Cameron was a keen advocate of carbon trading, looking to include it as part of the 'green deal' policy. Speaking at a Commonwealth conference, he stated his belief that carbon trading would fix 'the problem'.

Coronavirus resulted in the most significant drop in carbon emissions in recent history, but it was just a blip. The Met Office concluded in 2020 that the highest UK recorded temperature of some 35 C (July 2019) could be an annual event by 2100 at current rates: By 2050, London would then have the same climate as Istanbul.

What might really have been effective would have been a carbon tax, to equalise the private and social cost of releasing carbon. This has recently been implemented in Sweden with limited success. It was *regressive*, hitting the poorer hardest. Another peer-reviewed study by William Nordhaus concluded the 2 C target was unfeasible and that even reaching a 2.5 C target would require a $184 a tonne carbon tax compared with an estimated social cost of carbon of a mere $31 a tonne; a considerable shortfall.

I personally believe carbon trading to be a distraction from minimising the output of carbon emissions. 'Carbon Reduction Commitment' has lost its focus. In October 2010, the Treasury decreed that it would not ring-fence any further proceeds from subsidies to industry using renewable energy, the so-called *Renewable Heat Incentive*. It would go instead into the general tax pool like any other tax. Exceptionally, energy-intensive industries (such as steel and chemicals) are increasingly uneconomic because of the cost of carbon credit offsets. Oil and gas companies are also intending to pay for offsets in place of dealing with the emissions caused by refining their product: business as usual.

In this vein, non-renewable oil shale (fracking) is no answer. (We will be looking at this in a later chapter). The French government was the first to ban it. The Scottish government has allowed exploration, but only for a further year. In England and Wales, it was once encouraged; but currently, it looks unlikely. It is still uncertain what the upper limit of emissions the planet will tolerate staying at 2 C. Famines and floods continue to intensify. The atmosphere is now 4% more humid than thirty years ago, and this is shifting the jet stream. Arctic winter cyclones have continued to strengthen the polar vortex, causing extreme weather events in the mid-latitudes (further south than previously). USA temperatures are at more than 4.8 C hotter than the all-time average. The crowd-funded Fanny Adams film, *The Age of*

Stupid, came out around this time; highlighting these extremities. The findings underline the extent of the changes that human actions are wreaking on the planet. '...Melting of the Antarctic ice cap would continue even if the world met the Paris agreement goal of holding temperature rises to no more than 2 C, and would eventually raise sea levels by 2.5 metres at that level of heating.'

In order to plan for future risk reduction, two critical factors are paramount: population growth will continue to put more and more people in harm's way, while uncontrolled building on flood plains or storm-prone coastal zones will increase human vulnerabilities to extreme weather events.

Further *Committee of the Party* meetings failed to make much progress. Then the UK Labour government passed the *Climate Change Act;* and in 2016, the Paris agreement on human carbon dioxide was agreed upon by 21 countries. Now we have the *Extinction Rebellion*, Greta Thunberg, her *School strike for climate movement* and *Fridays for the Future.*

However, back in 2006, this had barely begun. Most non-governmental organisations (other than *Greenpeace*) were constrained by their charity status from taking direct action. The Labour party had, it seemed, long lost interest in the Green agenda. Politics could not move this issue forward, nor even the United Nations.

The climate sceptic lobby, funded by big oil and coal, had been hard at work sowing disinformation and confusion in the minds of a gullible American public: what we now know as fake news. The best known is the *Heartland Institute*, active in USA public school education programs. There seemed to be a belief among the oil lobby that the planet had no intrinsic value, a lack of respect reflected in their accountancy practices, which attribute no cost to nature, and threatened their businesses. In March 2007, Channel 4 itself became embroiled in so-called fake news, in airing a documentary, *The Great Global Warming Swindle*. Producer Martin Durkin came under fire for his selective use of quotes. Many contributors complained that their views had been misrepresented, and blatantly edited to a different petroleum agenda.

There is increased perception among investors that petroleum is a stranded asset. Disinvestment by arts bodies and pension funds continues. Politicians continue to be funded by them; under-fire Home Secretary Priti Patel is currently among the Tories who have been courted by the Global Warming Policy Foundation (GWPF), an industry lobby group that works to stymie policies against climate change. Their budget exceeds anything an environmental NGO can afford, but the tide is now turning. BlackRock signed up to Climate Action 100+, a pressure group of investors who are pushing the world's largest CO^2 emitters to cut funding. 'BlackRock does not see itself as a passive observer in the low-carbon transition.' In fact, it has \$7 trillion in assets. CEO Fink said, 'We believe we have a significant responsibility—as a provider of index funds, as a fiduciary, and as a member of society—to play a constructive role in the transition.' HSBC too, have pledged to phase out new coal project lending by 2040.

Even legal threats are looming. Exxon's past funding of climate denial has come home to roost. Internal documents reveal they knew as long ago as 1988 that their business was threatened by a wider knowledge of climate change. The

New York attorney general is charging the corporation with fraud. It is alleged that 'two sets of books' were kept. At trial, Exxon is expected to acknowledge it had two sets of carbon costs but is expected to argue investors should have known this, and how the different prices were used based on disclosures. The New York attorney general estimates the damage to Exxon shareholders ranges from about $476 million to $1.6 billion.

Enmeshed in a web of fossil-fuel dependency, prevarication continued. Carbon capture and storage would use a huge amount of energy. Nobody wanted to take unilateral action.

Neither can it be acceptable for advanced capitalist countries to place the burden for tackling climate change on the developing World, denying such newcomers the right to economic development. At the 2011 Durban COP, three big players: China, India and the USA had obstructed climate change mitigation, in the belief, it would jeopardise economic growth. The issue of differentiation is one of the main friction points: It holds that industrial and developing nations shouldn't have the same obligations because the poorer countries aren't as rich and need to focus resources on alleviating poverty. Governments had not been short of both advice and disinformation from climate scientists. It depended on who was paying. Dr James E. Hansen, Head of National Aeronautics and Space Administration at NASA's Goddard Institute, spoke up for the camp at Warwick University. Many scientists unfortunately lacked the media skills necessary to counter the fossil fuel lobby.

The result, he said, was that in recent years '…a gap had opened up between what is understood about global warming by the relevant scientific community, and what's known by the people who need to know – and that's the public. However, there's nothing that has happened to reduce 'our' scientific conclusion that we are pushing the system into very dangerous territory…'

While he was among the most vocal of scientists, he was not the only one to have written to then Prime Minister Gordon Brown about the urgency of the problem. *The Royal Society, Sir David King and the Centre for Alternative Technology* had all been lobbying. It all ended up on the desk of Sir Malcolm Wickes, minister in the newly formed Department for Business, Enterprise and Regulatory Reform.

In the UK, it would take until 2017 for solar power to provide nearly a quarter of the country's electricity needs, thanks to summer skies and relatively low summer demand, on 26 May. (National Grid confirmed that the solar power of thousands of photovoltaic panels, on rooftops and in fields across the UK, had generated 8.7GW, or 24.3% of demand at that time).

The problem with solar is that sunlight is normally too oblique for us in Northern Europe, except in high summer; when again it could be cloudy and too diffuse. The irony was that there has never been a shortage of energy in the world – daylight. It is just in the wrong place, often at the wrong time. 'Sunshine arrives free of charge at 14400 times the rate of global primary energy consumption.'

The equatorial latitudes, where it is strongest, are removed in both space and time from major population centres; local resources are easier to exploit than those a considerable distance away. Wholesale solar power prices reached another record low. In only two years, the cost of photovoltaics had nearly halved (from US$0.70 a watt in 2014 down to $0.45 two years later).

For India, the third-largest emitter, this has increased the odds of meeting the renewable energy target it had set itself at the *Paris Climate Accord* in December 2015. Analysts called the price drop 'world-historic', driven by cheaper finance and growing investor confidence in India, breaking the reliance on coal. The US and Europe are concerned that China and India hide behind differentiation to limit the action they must take against global warming.

Quoting from his 2009 book, *Storms of my Grandchildren*, James Hansen explained that for the planet to be in equilibrium, energy radiating should equal energy received. He worked with NASA's model for long-term climate projections. The Goddard Institute for Space Studies since 1988.

He affirmed his belief that humans had upset this balance. CO^2, methane and other gases absorb infrared from the planet's surface. There is little effect on the radiation coming in, but he believed it prevented heat from leaving at the same rate, causing a blanket effect around the earth.

He drew attention to positive feedback. As the planet becomes warmer, the larger area of darker water there will be, as ice sheets melt increase. Once started, this would take a millennium to return to equilibrium. There is amplifying feedback, As oceans become warmer, they give up dissolved CO^2 to the atmosphere and melted water absorbs more sunlight than snow.

'It is now clear we are exceeding our planet's support system. The rate of change is now 10,000 times faster than before the Industrial Revolution. Referring to changes since the last ice age, there will of course be natural changes, but humans are contributing to these cycles,' Dr Hansen believed.

Twenty percent of our earth's surface is permafrost – which is melting, releasing methane. The depth of the active layer—the layer of soil above permafrost that freezes in the winter and thaws in the summer—is believed to be increasing to varying degrees across sites, meaning the thaw is accelerating.

He warned of the effect of disintegrating ice sheets and inertia in the system already built-in. When the 'tipping point' is reached, these processes will become extreme. Whereas there is disagreement about the rates of change, there is a large agreement about the consequences. In Europe, large human populations living in low-lying maritime areas are at risk of inundation. In reality, ninety-three percent of the heat trapped by increasing greenhouse gases goes into warming the ocean, not the atmosphere. This causes water to expand, a threat that is most severe to low-lying coastal areas and islands.

'Coal is a problem fuel because stocks are so much larger than oil and gas reserves on the earth. With the approach of 'peak oil', oil and gas will become more expensive as it becomes more problematic to extract dwindling reserves.' No talk of 'peak coal' though. 'Burning coal is the dirtiest of fuels and should be left in the ground. We simply must phase out coal-burning for energy generation.' The prospect of carbon capture and storage remains a longer-term goal in the UK (but has failed to reach the pilot stage).

Both British and European governments subsidise coal-fired power station operators to ensure secure electricity supplies in winter. This ploy, designed 'to keep the lights on', has unfortunately served to undermine the floor price for carbon.

Coal is merely used at peak times. 'The coal sector (at that time) benefited from £356m a year in subsidies in the UK, despite the Government's pledge to phase out the use of the highly polluting fossil fuel,' a report relates; for just the three coal-fired stations still in use. REF Ten out of the twenty-seven European countries produce 84 percent of the EU's carbon dioxide emissions, according to the Overseas Development Institute (*ODI*). The international development think tank rated the UK as poor on transparency in relation to phasing out these subsidies, according to Shelagh Whitley, head of the climate and energy program there.

Nevertheless, the Government commitment to phasing out polluting coal-fired power plants by 2025 seems on track; Britain managed its first full day without coal generating any electricity since the nineteenth century in April 2018 and for 67 days continuously ending June 2020. It is, however, the consumer who is footing the bill with escalating energy costs.

In America, the world's largest storage battery system is being planned. It will distribute 900 megawatt-hours of electricity, in Florida's Manatee County. The FPL Energy Storage Centre is to replace two gas-fired power plants. In Australia, Elon Musk has offered to construct the world's largest lithium-ion battery at Jamestown. In Trafford Park near Manchester, a liquid air battery is under construction, it can power 200,000 homes for five hours. These battery projects all aim to even out daily fluctuations in demand.

By contrast, after pledging to close down its nuclear reactors by 2022, Germany has regressed to coal. That now provides more than a quarter of its electricity, to fill the base load vacated by nuclear energy. Renewable energy and gas provide the remainder. Germany accounted for more than £1.7bn in subsidies to coal (€2bn), while across the ten G20 countries, a mere 14% of the money identified as subsidies were being paid to support a transition away from fossil fuels. 'European countries need to phase out coal if they are to meet the Paris climate agreement targets, fight air pollution and support a change to low-carbon energy systems.' Only Spain is on track to achieve this. In Spain, a pledge to close down coal mining has led to ten pits shutting. Over one thousand workers will lose their jobs, but around 60% will be eligible for early retirement, and around 600 will receive social aid. The mines in question are private mines, but the government is beginning negotiations on a similar deal with the remaining few hundred miners in state mines.

The unloved Kyoto Agreement failed to lower emissions. It came into force on 16 February 2005. A number of developing countries (so-called 'Annexe 1') were also given targets to reduce emissions. The current, *Paris Climate Accord,* aims to stabilise emissions at 1990 levels. This is based on the principle of equity, which means that richer countries must lead by example. Kyoto took so long to be ratified by signatories, it was in place for just 7 years. There was a gap of four years until the Paris climate agreement was signed after the Copenhagen COP achieved nothing. Kyoto had to be ratified by 55 countries before it became legally binding on any. The quota system did derive in large measure from Aubrey Meyer's idea of *contraction and convergence*, a concept he put forward in the early 1990s. This envisaged that countries would reduce their greenhouse gas output and move toward some common point of equal emissions across the world. Each country was tasked with setting their 'Intended Nationally Determined Contributions'. The agreement to commit countries to a 5.6% cut in CO_2 emission relative to a 1990 baseline did not include Canada. The Canadian government had announced its intention to exploit oil tar sand and showed no willingness to become involved. Kyoto was fatally undermined because of the boycott by the USA and Canada (though China did sign up).

Kyoto had tied up progress at the annual United Nation's *Committee of Parties* meetings for many years. These 'talking shops' had met every year, with little concrete result to show for it. It would take until 2016 for the long-standing rift between developing and developed world interests to be resolved in Paris. Each country again had to agree on its own 'nationally determined contribution' (*NDC*) towards the common goal of limiting global warming.

To fulfil pledges they had made in Paris, nations must step up with new targets for emissions for 2030. Global carbon emissions are now 4% above the levels they were in 2015 when the Paris accord was signed. According to scientific advice, staying within 1.5 C would require a reduction of more than 7% a year for the next decade.

A survey of the new Nationally Determined Contributions (NDCs) that nations are due to submit before the next UN climate summit, the Glasgow COP26, shows that 32 of the 101 countries with net-zero targets have enhanced their NDC, compared with 11 of 90 countries without a net-zero target.

For its part, the UK has attempted to replace about a third of its existing electricity generating capacity, mainly coal and nuclear. The whole system had been privatised in 1998, which has hindered progress. That is an unprecedented and enormously expensive challenge, the cost of which was being passed back to consumers by the 'big six' with increased tariffs.

In Eastern Europe, in what was being alluded to as the new 'coal curtain', both output and consumption are increasing. The EU target to reach 20% renewables by 2020 was missed. Currently, it achieves 7% overall, a 14% shortfall on the target.

The *International Energy Agency* found that global carbon emissions rose in 2018, with a new fleet of coal plants in Asia accounting for a third of this increase. The *World Coal Association* said in a statement: 'As the largest source of electricity generation, coal will continue to be a critical enabler of development. For many countries, particularly in South and Southeast Asia, it underpins economic development. We must respect and support them in their choice and fund low emission technologies.' This is a particular issue for the USA and China to resolve if carbon is to be brought under control.

Existing US coal-fired electricity production still accounts for half of USA coal usage but is becoming increasingly uneconomic compared to new solar and wind energy. Additionally, even the best modern coal-fired still produce significantly more CO_2 than gas power stations.

Instead, consumers have had to pick up the cost of installing renewable energy on their metre tariff. As Bill McKibben of *350.org* in the USA had written: 'Change the price of energy to reflect the damage it does to the environment. If fossil fuel reflected that cost, we'd see these new systems and transitions happening much more rapidly. A cap on carbon that raises its price is a sine qua non for getting anything done'. This had also been the conclusion of the UK's Department of Energy and Climate Change's (*DECC*), but it hasn't happened.

In 2013, Britain alone consumed 200 million tonnes of oil equivalent (mtoe) of primary energy, of which gas was 33%, oil was 35%, and coal was 18%. It was into this background, came (Climate Camp).

The UK's nuclear power station stock is also ageing, largely run at reduced output owing to reactor and boiler plant deterioration with loss of reliability. In the UK, nuclear currently provides a substantial 27% of the base load to power our national grid, from 8 power stations. Nuclear power is electricity produced whatever the weather. It caused a rift in the camp, and it is pertinent to look at the reasons why (next chapter).

Chapter 4

The Nuclear Power Conundrum

There are now 440 nuclear reactors in operation worldwide, with around 60 more proposed or under construction. Nuclear was described by its own lobby group as '...the only viable source of low-carbon base load power available to industrialised economies'. Nuclear power was, however, vilified by many campers, some veterans of CND and Greenham Common, who had campaigned against nuclear missiles. Many journalists, like Mark Lynas, claimed that more than a billion tonnes of CO^2 emissions per year could be avoided (if nuclear power was expanded) Many sites, some existing, some new, were under investigation and a shortlist of eight was eventually published in June 2011 (the *Nuclear National Policy Statement*).

Chris Huhne, a former energy minister, also had reservations. He stated that 'Britain is still paying for nuclear-generated electricity consumed a generation ago because of the hidden costs of an industry reared on the expectation of public subsidies'. He told the *Royal Society* in London that the nuclear industry and the Government should show that they have learned from their past mistakes if they are to retain public support for a renaissance in nuclear power. And some of those mistakes are not small,' he said in his keynote address. 'Nuclear policy is a runner to be the most expensive failure of post-war British policy-making, and I am aware that this is a crowded and highly contested field.'

He was referring to the uniquely British advanced gas-cooled reactor design, which had proved uneconomic compared to water-cooled competitors, and slower to bring into service. The British never trusted water as a coolant. British-designed reactors were all gas-cooled. The *Boiling water* and *pressurised water* reactors which now dominate international design are all water-cooled.

They also failed to sell abroad even though they were claimed to be safer; which might have brought economies of scale.

Current plans for the electricity market are intended to address this risk liability, by means of *contracts for difference*, in which generators contract to supply power at a price above the market rate were 'pioneering' and '...ensure continuing reliability of electricity systems while promoting timely de-carbonisation of electricity supplies', at no initial cost to the taxpayer. This is the cradle-to-grave funding model used for the Hinkley Point nuclear power station. Huhne was also alluding to the end product, nuclear waste – what to do with it, and how much it was going to cost to deal with it. Plutonium and tritium can only be created through fission, essential components for nuclear bombs. It also creates hundreds of radionuclides, needing to be cooled for thousands of years.

Two atomic piles at Sellafield were crucial to Britain's atomic weapon program. They used uranium oxide fuel rods to make the required plutonium, finned alloy tubes inserted in a massive block of graphite with air-cooling. An accidental fire in 1957 came close to a meltdown, causing national panic. Milk had to be discarded. Scientists had been forced by Cold War government pressure to rush the full-scale implementation of technology they had only just developed. Subsequently, sealed containment vessels were employed after the accident and electricity generated. These early reactors had the great advantage of running on un-enriched uranium (0.7% of $U^{235)}$ in magnesium alloy tubes.

This liquid carbon dioxide cooled MAGNOX design then went into small batch production to generate sufficient bomb-making material under the 'atoms for peace' moniker. The civilian power program also came to have a covert political role in curbing the power of the National Union of Mineworkers.

One of the greatest risks at these plants is the amount of spent fuel stored on-site, which requires cooling via electrically driven water pumps, before being shunted back by rail to Sellafield. If the pumps fail, the water will evaporate in short order, the remaining heat generated will melt the surrounding rods and release radioactive contaminants into the atmosphere. If the power is out, there will be little to no warning and since you can't smell, taste or see it, this could happen quickly.

The MAGNOX power station at Trawsfynydd in North Wales was one of the early prototypes. It was powered up in 1965, a scaled-up version of Calder Hall's original. It did, however, not run for long at a design potential of 470MW. Due to a string of technical difficulties, it could only be run at reduced power.

While it may have only cost £120 million (in 1959 prices) to build, it has cost £800 million to de-commission. This is considered by the industry to be the cheapest decommissioning so far. No thought had been given in the original design as to how it could be dismantled. Robots had to be developed, which could cut up the internal containment vessel remotely.

For the brief 26 years of its generating life, it was dogged by technical problems and hairline cracking of the containment vessels. It was the only nuclear power station ever built in the UK above sea level. It was cooled with lake water and went on to contaminate the Trawsfynydd lakebed, mainly with Caesium-137.

According to official documents, this will decay to a safe level in another 15 years. However longer-lived elements (including plutonium) escaped in the 1970s from the spent fuel pool, and have settled on the lake bottom.

So was it economical? Electricity production was, in any case, secondary to plutonium production. The waste returned to Sellafield, would have the plutonium for extraction from the spent rods (about 1% by weight). The uranium would then be refreshed and available for new fuel rods. The re-processing results in toxic releases to the Irish Sea, with more dangerous fission products destined for a permanent repository yet to be built. By 1995 Britain had more than enough plutonium for its weapons program, and its safe storage (above ground) an ongoing expense. It is currently being turned into glass. These future costs are not included in de-commissioning the existing.

The UK Government did not want to fund nuclear power, for the first time, operators of new nuclear plants in the UK will have to pay upfront for the entire capital cost (including decommissioning). Then the energy companies will buy it back; the consumer will pay. This is what makes nuclear power so uneconomic compared to renewables. It is PFI. It still falls to the UK government to find a suitable geological disposal site. It aims to ensure that it will be the nuclear power operators—and not taxpayers—who bear the cost of disposing of their nuclear waste and that they had set aside sufficient funds to cover these future liabilities. This deal was designed to circumvent EU rules about state aid. Bidders were under an obligation to set aside sufficient funds to cover their future liabilities. The European Commission agreed that the anticipated disposal costs were realistic. Operators would also have to pay a proportionate risk fee to benefit from the cap. The 'big six' would buy the power on a 'pay as you go' basis.

The big unknown remains the actual cost of disposal (around 30 years after the start of the power station). 'The UK Government has always wanted to build a geological facility for the disposal of spent fuel and intermediate-level waste from existing and new nuclear power stations in the UK.' They have so far failed to find a site with sufficient geological stability and political acceptability. The Radioactive Waste Management facility needs to start operating around 2075 and fill up by 2140. This facility would likely be the only geological disposal site in the UK in the foreseeable future.

The argument for this form of energy was only brought forward in the 1990s. It is purely that it *could* be a low CO^2 technology capable of great energy intensity. This was an entirely new argument, while in 1960, it was just another way to generate electricity, with a facile promise that it would be 'too cheap to metre!' In considering the power required for uranium mining and especially enrichment, it is unclear whether the lifecycle carbon footprint could compare with renewable energy. Then we have the intractable life of the waste problem.

Since Chernobyl, Three Mile Island and now Fukushima, the consequences of containment failure can be devastating. The dreaded 'China syndrome', where the melted core, at many thousand deg C, continues to burn through the foundations can eventually reach the water table.

The industry has attempted recycling – the spent fuel rods can have trace fission products cleaned out, all the time creating all sorts of transuranic elements. Some of these have ended up in the Irish Sea. Nuclear fuel can be re-used when the fission products have been removed. In addition, enriched uranium is available from decommissioned bombs. The UK had hoped to stretch supplies further by the use of MOX (a mixture of uranium and plutonium).

It succeeded in re-using a mere 13 tonnes of plutonium, but it turned out to be another costly technical failure. The £1 340 million Thorp plant had to be abandoned. To put it unkindly, the fuel it produced cost the taxpayer £100+ million per tonne of fuel rods manufactured.

It is tragic that one of the four reactors which melted down at Fukushima (No. 3) was fuelled with the mixed oxide fuel rods from Sellafield. Plutonium (with a half-life of 25,000 years) was vaporised.

Sellafield is currently re-processing 200 tonnes per year of spent uranium for Japanese and UK government customers, at reduced capacity. Of the four nuclear power stations that were proposed; only Hinkley Point C is under construction. It is already over budget, and it is unclear when it will finally be generating electricity.

Chapter 5

The Policing of the Camps

The police in the UK generally base their theories of crowd control on the theory of Le Bon, a Frenchman. This is known as *policing by consent.* Robert Peel was the Victorian who carried this through in the metropolitan area. Laws, like good policing, should rely on our consent. So perhaps the best advice is mostly to follow such rules, but always to ask why. Elsewhere, including France, a more confrontational position tends to be the norm, as in many other countries with a history of communist or fascist rule.

Crowds everywhere are seen as inherently dangerous because of the potential threat they may pose to the status quo and need to be contained and/or controlled to prevent the disorder from spreading. While the majority of crowd members are perceived as peaceful, law-abiding citizens, they can be '…susceptible to being influenced by a *violent minority…*' to quote John Pilger: 'Using totalitarian laws approved by a majority of MP's, the police have set up secretive units to combat democratic dissent they call (domestic) extremism. This manipulation and disruption of protest is the main undercover officer focus.' We shall look further at domestic extremism in Chapter 14.

As Alistair Cooke wrote, 'If violence is a special sickness of our age, it is universal and nobody so far has come up with a cure.' According to the police *Code of Ethics*, '…force can be used to the extent that it is necessary, proportionate and reasonable in all the circumstances.'

'What is consent for some may be an imposition for others.' '…Protesting crowds are usually united in their desire for a change of some sort and this can cause them to be opposed by the apparatus of the state, of which the Police are a part.' Therefore, there always exists the potential for conflict between the two parties, even if it doesn't actually 'kick off'. While psychologists and sociologists recognise the potential crowds may enable society to change for the better, it is problematic for the Police. What we are talking about is the policing of public expression in an era of economic change.

Their current guidelines are set out in the *Manual of Guidance on keeping the Peace*, which was first published in 2009. This was further updated in February 2011, prompted by misuse at Kingsnorth Climate Camp, and a successful civilian claim connected with stop and search powers there. During the review, it has become clear that a number of police officers/commanders have approached peaceful protest in terms of 'is the protest lawful/unlawful?' So wrote Her Majesty's Inspectorate of Constabulary (HMIC). 'A better approach is to consider how to facilitate the peaceful protest.'

As the camps continued, Police evolved new strategies in an attempt to *pre-empt* any criminal activity that might be committed. They did this by the extensive use of the stop and search powers available to them under the *Criminal Justice*

Act of 1994. The common law offence of 'unlawful assembly' had been abolished in the *Public Order Act* of 1986, because of the acceptance of civilian protest rights and EU human rights policy. The camp frequently overstepped what the police understood to be acceptable behaviour and this was frustrating for both sides.

Things became more hard-core the nearer the campers got to London. Here, after a series of violent assaults on officers in the 1990s, the Met had militarised their approach to street protest, relative to the rest of the country outside London. 'They dressed officers in new, military-style uniforms, gave them anti-stab vests and equipped them with equipment like extendable metal batons and clubs that turn into handcuffs'. The 720 strong *Territorial Support Group* (*TSG*) specialise in public order containment…it replaced the former Special Patrol Group in 1987. Officers in this group are identified by the letter 'U' on their shoulder lapels. Some are ex-military personnel.

Officers are trained to believe that they are continually under physical threat and must therefore be continually 'on their guard'. It appeared to me that a significant minority of officers saw the public as their enemy, and as a potential hazard to be dealt with aggressively. But no senior officer has been reprimanded for this policy, although several junior ranks have been charged over the years. It seems this is acceptable to the Home Office. Sir Paul Stevenson, then commander of the Metropolitan Police at that time, resigned, but only because of an entirely unrelated issue, of illegal phone tapping.

The magistrate's court found PC Simon Harwood 'not guilty' for the unlawful killing of Ian Tomlinson. The trial took place despite an earlier decision by the coroner (July 2010) that no charge could be brought, for lack of causal evidence.

This all changed when evidence on the contrary surfaced. The *Guardian* newspaper published a mobile phone video taken by New York business executive Christopher La Jaunie. Simon Harwood was then sacked; even the coroner was struck off. Following these events, relations between police and activists at subsequent camps improved as the police adopted a more 'hands-off' model. However, continued use of kettling, even on a peaceful NHS march, has reminded the public that protest can come at a personal cost. (Refer to Chapter 15)

The National Union of Journalists, the *NUJ*, called for then Home Secretary Jacqui Smith to put an end to police surveillance of journalists on the basis that they were not participants. That move came after evidence that the Metropolitan Police Forward Intelligence Team (*FIT*) had been videoing journalists, especially photographers. Some had come across their details from the database using the *Freedom of Information Act*. Anyone can ask this for a £10 fee.

Their Freedom of Information requests had revealed that the 'Crimint' database holds large amounts of information on persistent protesters, information kept for at least seven years. Police stressed that the only reason these tactics were necessary was because protesters would not 'engage' with the police pre-event. All demonstrations were supposed to be cleared with the police in advance, they said.

'If the protesters will not talk to us, well…we can't just police the event – by definition, we're caught in the middle because we're seen as the physical manifestation of the state because we wear uniforms and we go around in white trucks.'

The *Open Democracy website* asked whether it could be that police enjoy having a degree of flexibility in interpreting the law. It gives their officers loose rein to arrest anyone they deem a nuisance, even when they know their case could collapse before the courts, given there is no such offence as 'domestic extremism'?

Writer Paul Rogers had this to say: 'The political challenge posed by non-violent direct action (NVDA) on climate change has three aspects. The first is that the long tradition of peaceful protest in Britain—preceding even the landmark anti-nuclear mobilisations of the *Committee of* 100 in the 1960s—had focused mostly on opposition to military policy, but has the potential to influence wider public attitudes. The campaigns directed at military bases—such as the *Faslane 365* campaign against Britain's main nuclear-missile base in western Scotland–have had an impact, in Scotland especially, but the authorities can still protect such military facilities from non-violent demonstrators with relatively little difficulty. It is harder, however, to contain the exemplary and symbolic impact of campaigns of this kind'. The second aspect is that this form of protest does have the potential to cause real disruption. Coal deliveries to Britain's largest power station at Drax, in North Yorkshire, were disrupted in June 2008. (29 persons charged, on 13 June 2008) The obstruction of a coal train en route to the power station; the *Malicious Damage Act 1861* was invoked.

The enforced closure of the Stansted Airport in December 2008 was another example. Such actions are significant in that airports, power stations, the road network and other potential targets are widely dispersed. The private sector needed intelligence as much (if not more so than) as the police. Companies including Scottish Power, E.On and Scottish Resources Group (*SRG*), which owns Scottish Coal, were also revealed to have employed a 'risk management company' to keep tabs on activists' moves.

Even a few hundred protesters in the right place can have a major impact, and greater numbers with the knowledge and analytical skills to identify the key weak points in Britain's economy (especially its energy-distribution systems) could create chaos through a program of coordinated actions.

A European-wide electrical blackout in 2006 demonstrated the fragility of interconnected power systems. A single disconnect of a high-tension power line led to a continent-wide power cut. On a Saturday morning on 4 November a power line over the river Ems in Northwest Germany was switched off, to allow a tall ship to pass safely beneath the high-tension cables. Within 28 seconds, an electrical blackout cascaded right across Europe. It extended from Poland in the northeast, to the Benelux countries and France in the west, through to Portugal, Spain and even across to Morocco in the south-west; and to Greece and the Balkans in the southeast. The fourth aspect is the experience of September 2000, when a UK-wide dispute involving fuel-tanker drivers nearly brought the country to an effective standstill in a matter of days. It left motorists stranded wherever they happened to run out of fuel. This traumatic event, in the otherwise still relatively popular government of Tony Blair, caused significant public alarm. It highlighted the vulnerability of our modern interconnected economy.

A selective but nationwide, English electrical blackout recurred in 2019, albeit for a mere few hours. This was allegedly caused by a lightning strike on power lines, leading to the failure of two generators tripping within two minutes of each other. That meant hospitals blacked out and electric trains brought to a halt.

These factors help explain the government's and the police's strong reaction to the eruption of protest. Non-violent direct action has in the post-1945 era acquired an extraordinary pedigree arising from numerous campaigns worldwide.

It in fact seems protest has become the preferred continuation of politics by other means. Indeed, 2011 was titled *Year of the Protester* by Time Magazine.

The issue confronting the Climate Camp was how to combine openness within and security outside. This conundrum was never resolved. Moral panics, created or set up deliberately by the state' the 'false flag' event, were used by the police as a means of gathering intelligence. The threat of violence is an essential marker in overturning the scant protection afforded by the EU Court of human rights, on the definition of a criminal offence. Violence against the person was the subject of a select committee on undercover policing.

Brighton Green party MP Caroline Lucas had this to say to the select committee: 'The *Regulation of Investigatory Powers Act 2000* (*RIPA*), is the legislative framework that enables police and other public authorities using covert human intelligence sources, such as undercover officers, to ensure that they act in compliance with the Human Rights Act. A "overt human intelligence source" is the term used for a member of a law enforcement agency who infiltrates organisations planning disruption or criminal acts'. The supervisor of an undercover agent (UCO) is termed a COM-UC, an officer of at least inspector rank, who is responsible for an undercover unit. These are the people who set the parameters of what their undercover officers can do. They are both judge and jury. There was to be no ban on covert operatives having sex with a target, Home Office Minister Nick Herbert stated, (unlike Germany, where it is). Apparently, police chiefs and inspectors thought this was *because it would give potential criminals an easy test to find out whether someone was who they said they were!* He continued: '...*I am not persuaded* that it would be appropriate to issue specific statutory guidance under RIPA about sexual relationships' (quoted in *Hansard*). Yet no principles regarding the police use of potentially sensitive information which may later become evidence in legal proceedings still unresolved. Since then, the Metropolitan police have had to compensate a number of women who found themselves in compromised relationships.

Mark Stone (real name) travelled to eleven countries at 'government expense' to gather information about activists. In France, he infiltrated a group of left-wing activists living in the remote village of Tarnac and gathered evidence that saw them accused of an alleged terrorist plot to overthrow the state.

The 2009 Climate Camp event did influence police strategy, and following the death of Ian Tomlinson a year later, led the change to the strategy manual, *Keeping the Peace*. This introduced the less confrontational policing strategy of *no surprises*.

Meanwhile, Greta Thunberg has spoken truth to power—now being serialised by the BBC—more effectively than anyone before. As a mere teenager, she has frequently been attacked by male politicians, who have accused her of being a pawn of larger interests. Bernier in Canada is but one typical example. Behind the poster girl image, there must surely be a high-profile support team. How much 'science' Greta actually knows remains uncertain, but she is not short of advice. In the background are powerful interests. Louisa-Marie Neubauer, a 23-year-old German 'climate protection' activist in the Strike for Climate Movement. She supports the implementation of *Agenda 2030* in Germany, with the Alliance 90/The Greens and the Green Youth, but also belongs to a far-left organisation called *One Foundation*. According to *Deutschland-Kurier*, she is their 'Youth Ambassador'. Are these the kids of the elite on their first global green gig? Family links to Sandvik, AREVA and Rio Tinto have been cited, companies with licenses worldwide to build more nuclear power plants, aided by this global public-relations exercise.

The world's largest institutional investors, including BlackRock and Goldman Sachs, the UN, the World Bank, the Bank of England and other central banks, have lined up behind the financing of a so-called green Agenda, call it *Green New Deal* or whatever, it is time to ask about the actual agenda. It amounts to the financial reorganisation of the world economy-using climate. The Green bandwagon is now big business. Climate change is a global industry on which livelihoods and reputations depend. Take Tesla, for example.

The pushback had started. Naomi Seibt took the opposing position. She spoke at The Heartland Institute and at the

Conservative Political Action Conference (CPAC) in Maryland to about a hundred delegates. She has dismissed allegations that she is a 'puppet of the right-wing or the climate deniers or the Heartland Institute either.'

On 3 December 2019, she spoke (the only woman invited to an event that is 'traditionally dominated by older men') at the Madrid 'Climate Reality Forum', a forum organised to rebut the United Nations' climate change warnings. Germany's AfD had embraced climate change denial, as part of their nationalist political campaign in Europe. Perhaps because they felt safer in denial, their tension resolved by rejecting the evidence.

At the same time, Greta Thunberg was speaking at the 2019 United Nations Climate Change Conference (COP25) several miles away. Movements started by children can gather momentum and enact change, and now adults need to take on board Thunberg's refreshing enthusiasm and 'can-do' attitude and apply it to practical solutions in science and engineering.

Chapter 6

The Truth Is Out There – Beyond Fossil Fuel

Certainly, I believe, there was unanimity among everyone at the camp that fossil fuels were, if not solely responsible for global warming, the most important – the target of their efforts. We discounted other sources that had always been there; from volcanoes to agriculture.

'We remain exceedingly dependent on the natural environment that surrounds us, and that natural environment is becoming increasingly unstable.' In 2020, a spring in lockdown, this has become obvious, road traffic pollution reduced to 1920s levels.

'Environmental campaigners often struggle to convince the wider public about the need to combat climate change. Whilst most people agree with the *principle* of protecting the environment in the abstract, they are suspicious of many of the suggestions that environmentalists put forward to tackle the problem of climate change, ''I is also due however to the nature of the proposals, which tend to consist of higher taxes, more regulation and greater government spending. It is not practical to take on board such policies without the necessary consensus to implement them. Since climate change is a long-term problem (albeit with short-term effects), it is difficult to convey the need for instant action, so the focus shifts to the negative aspects of the plan (higher taxes), as well as the continued growth in emissions in places like China.' (It was at this time that China was reported to be opening a new coal-fired power station every ten days).

In point of fact, it is still unclear what proportion of the problem has been caused by fossil fuels, and how much is caused by de-afforestation and intensive agriculture. The ruling philosophy is now: support anything that reduces CO^2, climate science limits. Indeed, The Chinese government has recently slashed its solar and wind subsidies by \$117.6 billion, causing a sharp fall in the number of new projects worldwide. The disappearance of 39 percent of China's funding amounted to a 14 percent drop in global renewable investment.

However, with a nod to the global concerns, it has since then vowed to become zero-carbon by 2060 (October 2020).

Accounting methods need to be updated, to include 'costing the earth'. The traditional asset valuation method assigns costs to land, capital and labour; problems that arise from pollution or the environment are not considered to cost anything. This means the cost of using a resource is currently nil (apparently).

The European Union continues to subsidise biofuels, in the blind belief that because they are not petroleum-based, they must sequester carbon; in the similar mistaken way, it did for diesel. The biofuel industry lobby group has become big business, a successful lobby that depends on the EU. There now appears to be a concerted effort by its members and many of its proponents to equate climate change emissions solely with reducing fossil fuel emissions, to disregard or downplay consequential emissions from the destruction of forests, grasslands, peatlands and previously diverse agricultural systems with high biodiversity, and thereby suggest that anything that reduces fossil fuel burning must be good for the climate.

Nothing could be further from the truth. This is a more extreme version of the 'shifting the burden' archetype...whereby the symptomatic solution of fossil fuel carbon accounting takes precedence over the fundamental solution of addressing full lifecycle emissions. Simply put, in the name of reducing fossil fuel burning, global warming is actually being accelerated. This new and dangerous development requires a clear response from all climate change activists and means that we need to revisit our own thoughts regarding fossil fuel carbon versus biological carbon...It has ignored the destruction of carbon sinks such as indigenous forests on which they were planted over.

The amount of carbon that is added to the atmosphere is the difference between the quantity emitted and that absorbed by ecosystems. With current estimates of just over 50% of global emissions being absorbed by land and sea ecosystems, clearly sinks as well as emissions are equally important factors. At present, carbon trading provides funding for 'afforestation and re-afforestation', which unfortunately has generally meant monoculture tree-plantations: oil palm. These often have a devastating negative impact both socially and on biodiversity. The original *Kyoto* protocol did not provide finance for protecting existing forests; but the *Coalition for Rainforest Nations* aims to raise large sums of funds for conserving tropical forests, much of it via carbon trading mechanisms. The current proposal (2012) is for a Clean Development Mechanism, in which a combination of emissions trading and a fund for protecting existing forests alone is proposed. [xxx] The *Verified Carbon Standard* and the *Climate, Community and Biodiversity Standard* are both current models. The Clean Development Mechanism allowed rich countries to offset their emissions by buying carbon credits from emissions reduction or clean energy projects in 'poorer' countries.

This massive biodiversity loss in the tropics is a loss of carbon sinks. Every year, an area of forest equivalent to the size of Italy is lost. Previously diverse forest systems are usually destroyed by fire; for timber, for ranching, for soya or palm oil monoculture. Scientists reported that 17% of the Amazon rainforest has been lost since 1970. Up to 70% of the world's biodiversity is found in just 17 'mega-diverse' countries. Thirteen of these have tropical forests. In 2018 alone, these countries lost almost 7.3 million hectares of forests 14 – *an area roughly the size of Panama*. According to estimates (Nature), that represented nearly 30% of global deforestation and may have released about 7% of worldwide carbon emissions. A carbon tax policy could reduce the use of oil, gas and coal and mobilise domestic funds for adaptation and mitigation. A cleared forest can no longer absorb carbon when used for grazing. In 2019, fires lit in Brazil in the dry season by ranchers seeking to extend pasture got out of control, with tacit government support. Continued tropical deforestation (business as usual) is widely expected to release between 87-130 billion tonnes of carbon between now and 2107. PricewaterhouseCoopers LLP predicted that on current projections, the world would exceed an estimated 'carbon emissions budget' for the first half of this century by 2034, sixteen years ahead of the predicted schedule. In one of his lectures, Hansen even compared climate change to slavery.

Peatland restoration is already being used as a *carbon-offset* buffer for Heathrow Airport. Peat covers 12% of the landmass of the UK and a great deal more elsewhere. The world's peatlands are thought to contain between 180 to 455 billion metric tonnes of sequestered carbon, and they release 20 to 45 million metric tonnes of methane annually into the atmosphere. 'The opportunity is absolutely massive,' enthused environmentalist Tony Juniper, who unveiled Heathrow's new 'offsetting' plan. 'The vast majority of peat bogs are degraded and…releasing billions of tonnes of carbon over decades.'…their restoration would also benefit flood prevention and wildlife, according to the CEO of BAA, John Holland-Kaye. Offsetting is not a given, it has to be audited to be effective.

The EU aim with bio-fuels remains to reach 10% substitution this year. While this may marginally reduce CO2, it is, however, likely to result in an increase in carcinogens and nitrogen oxides, with implicit air quality implications for human health. It is not good for engine health either.

This same skewed offsetting is used to justify the clear-cutting of North Carolina forests for woodchip to be shipped all the way across the Atlantic to the Yorkshire Drax power station. The subsidy has distorted common sense. The 'shifting the burden' archetype has taken precedence over full life-cycle emissions; moving the deckchairs.

By 2010, the European Union had, amidst a community-wide recession, failed to motivate its members to reduce greenhouse gas emissions – with a number of member states either unable or unwilling to implement the directive. Severe winters always see a marked increase in emissions in any case. The problem was coal in Eastern Europe. While the UK had gone more than 3,000 hours in 2018-19 without using coal for power – nearly five times more than the whole of 2017, many eastern countries of the EU rely largely on coal for power generation.

Some, like Poland, and even Germany, burn massive amounts of lignite, mostly to generate electricity, very low-quality stuff; while Eire burns peat, another massive CO_2 source. There is a large gas pipeline (Nordstream-2) coming in from Russia being laid in the Baltic, which will help Germany to substitute gas for coal. While that country has many wind farms, it had also switched from nuclear to coal, to appease the anti-nuclear lobby, a political decision with negative carbon implications (and the target of the 2008 camp). In the USA, corn ethanol is a bio-fuel additive, which turns out to have a huge indirect carbon footprint, contribute to soil degradation and burnt-out car engines alike. These have merely been crops planted on land which could be growing crops.

Some countries with tropical forests have adopted a carbon tax – in South and Central America, Africa, Asia and the Pacific. These are paid for by a levy on fossil fuels that is invested in natural climate solutions. Elsewhere, Sweden has introduced a carbon tax, for which there seems to have been scant public support.

'Only in the last hundred years, with the invention of the internal combustion engine and a huge increase in population, has man begun to tap the planet's long-term energy supplies of oil and natural gas at an alarming rate. In merely a blink of an eye, we have shaped a world where our lifestyles revolve around and are dependent on oil and the consumption of energy from fossil fuels.' There are over 260 million vehicles in America alone, with more than a billion around the world, releasing gigantic quantities of carbon dioxide and other toxins into the environment each year. By contrast, there were a mere three million electric vehicles in use globally in 2019. The British car pool is 18.8 million, of which only 89000 were all-electric in 2018 (0.005%).

In fairness, the misconception that diesel was greener came from an earlier obsession with sequestrating CO^2 in the '90s, an idea popular with the Labour government. This is a mere 15% reduction in carbon compared to petrol. However, apart from a lower CO^2 output, diesel does not make a lot of sense – particulates (one hundred times more) and nitrogen oxides in volume. We now know it has been causing respiratory issues from the beginning, but it wasn't a mainstream idea at the time (except in the car industry). Instead, diesel was encouraged by a reduction in fuel duty. The EU responded by agreeing to cut the CO^2 output of new cars by 30% by 2030, with the rollout of the E6 testing program.

The *International Energy Association* said that the UK needed a more competitive energy market. It commended government plans for a 'green deal' to encourage households to insulate their homes, but warned that its success would depend on making the *public* 'sufficiently aware of its benefits'. In 2013, the National Audit Office in the UK concluded that the Department of Energy and Climate Change's (DECC) had failed. The £240 million *Green Deal* of 2011 has been money largely wasted. David Thorpe, an independent consultant, adversely compared the British approach to the successful German scheme and argued that a replacement is urgently needed. The UK scheme has not been replaced and was terminated in 2015.

So what went wrong? The *Green Deal* was an example of a 'Pay-as-you-save' type scheme; it came with no target or grants (unlike the German model, described below). Pricey loans were offered to householders to pay for the energy efficiency measures and repaid over time from the financial savings created by these measures. The 'Golden Rule' was that costs must be covered by savings over 25 years. The use of a 7-10% interest rate on the finance package was unpopular for most householders – many percentage points above the base rate at that time. The *Green Deal Finance* was also a charge attached to the property and recouped through premium charges on the electricity bill (even if the savings were made on a different fuel, say gas). So it could encumber the next purchaser too, if not fully termed.

Though 300,259 *Green Deal* assessments took place, only 15,000 'live' plans were implemented – a conversion rate of just 5% and a mere 1% took out the pricey finance option. Unpaid finance becomes a charge should the property be sold. There has been no replacement policy – and fuel poverty continues; had it been set up to fail? In Germany, by contrast, a million old homes have been retrofitted and 400,000 new highly efficient homes built (and this is a new build, not just a retrofit scheme). This is more than 9000 times as many as in Britain. The UK scheme was abolished in 2015, to eventually be replaced by the Green Homes Grant, which was scrapped after only six months. 'We won't reach net-zero through poorly designed policy initiatives.'

Greenpeace had this to say: 'The *Green Deal* was far from being a success, but coming right after the scrapping of the zero-carbon homes target, this latest move suggests ministers are giving up on efficiency. This would be a false economy. Fixing our heat-leaking homes is a triple-win policy that can bring down bills, cut carbon emissions, and reduce our dependence on energy imports.' (UK head of energy) In Germany, by contrast, the interest rate had been a more manageable 1–4%. Their 'EnEv' program, implemented from 1 February 2002, would loan up to €50,000 from State bank KfW for replacement of the heating and domestic hot water systems of a residence (and ventilation and cooling systems installed earlier than 2009).

The goal here is to use public policy to refurbish the entire housing stock and all public buildings in Germany by 2030. The outcome was a reduction in annual energy consumption by 900 GW hours and saved energy worth €150m per year.

To achieve 2050 carbon emission reduction targets, the UK's 28 million domestic properties would, according to David Thorpe, need to be renovated at a rate of 700,000 a year in order to have renovated them all by the year 2050. They also need to be renovated to a high standard, what might be termed a 'deep retrofit'.

This could involve replacing all gas-fired central heating. One suggestion is that boilers could be converted to run on hydrogen. Another is replacement with a microwave water heater. Neither is ready for market. No new timescale has been proposed.

It is however a clear sign that fossil fuels are on the way out.

Chapter 7

How the Camps Were Run

The need to assemble is a constant among humans. (We are social animals). Assembling corresponds to the joy of feeling a common power. As it was for *Occupy*, so it was for the camp. The camp was a way of life. You had to live in the present, launch yourself on every wave, and find your eternity in each moment.

The camps were fully functioning, highly pre-planned pop-up settlements held annually. Everything that was needed had to be brought to the site for that week, in little pieces for site assembly. The main structures arrived with the site 'swoop', with marquees designated as a workshop, entertainment, or kitchen zones provided by the national group. Accommodation and catering tents were provided by groups arriving from around the country.

Information was made freely available in advance on the (now no longer accessible) website *climatecamp.org.uk*. The organisers of the camp were keen to pass their responsibilities on to the participants, and in this, they were successful. This was a collective responsibility on-site. These individuals (the 'us') had a significant social investment in collaboration and social identification. The downside was that there was no safety net, no insurance, and no effective governance. The location of the Climate Camp was privy to a closed core group (or so we were told), the inner circle.

Self-contained communities were grouped geographically in 'barrios'. These neighbourhoods were separated by fire lanes. I take it to be no different from a circus community – decisions were made 'bottom up'. The nature of this *shared experience* led to a strong sense of community, and a special dynamic; just about sustainable for one week in August. The broader intention was to develop a social movement around the country; sadly, this was never realised. The technical edge was site power (wind, pedal and solar), the media (satellite up-link, radio, cinema and, later, a *YouTube* studio).

Pre-planning took place in the months preceding; rather than on the site. Each camp took six months to plan. Monthly meetings were central to this process. The Process group requested agenda items two weeks in advance, the facilitation-working group mentored those meetings ('facilitation').

The local council obviously had health and safety concerns. The issue of public liability insurance was simply swept under the carpet. It was not insurable. The issues of water (paid for), electricity (we made our own), toilets, hygiene, first aid and fire precautions were, however, all resolved. Fresh-piped water came from fire hydrants, electricity from shared solar panels and wind turbines. Local authority health inspectors inspected plumbing to the water supply.

Extensive use was made of recycled materials, mostly on cost (but also moral) grounds – items such as pallets and straw bales. Many structures, such as toilet seat platforms, were also prefabricated for speed of erection. The groups made their own decisions in whatever way they chose. The delegated issues included: Marquees, Transport, Power, Kitchens, Toilets, Liaison, Comms, Defence, Plumbing, Visuals, and Grey water.

The site entrance was linked to the main marquee by a wheelchair friendly track linking the neighbourhoods and the disabled access toilet. Forestry Stewardship Council certified (FSC) plywood sheets were used for walkways. Even induction loops were set up for people with hearing difficulties during meetings in the main marquee. On-site communications were sophisticated: a mixture of short-wave walkie-talkies and mobile phones.

The Comms tent was primarily concerned with walkie-talkie training, charging batteries; and site communication. The gate crew managed the primary communication, liaising with the tranquillity team; guarding entry points to the site, observing and reporting what the cops were up to.

Eleven field kitchens served three meals a day in tents. Calor gas for cooking was bought by individual groups. Ten of these were run by regional neighbourhoods. The overall one was the central kitchen, the first to be set up. All cooked food on site was vegan, most of which was organic. The central kitchen had a dedicated team from Common Place, (the Leeds social centre), which coordinated food ordering and storage throughout the camp. (Too short on protein for me). The central kitchen was divided from the dining space, using counters and tables. The back of the kitchen was full of pallets (to keep food off the ground) and in the middle space pans and cleaning equipment. The burners were located in the far corner, away from the general flow of people. Cooling could be achieved with water.

This kitchen, first-call for visitors, was a backup for the neighbourhoods. It coordinated the cooking, staggered the timing of meals and suggested menus. Each person needs half a litre of food per meal. By the time we reached Kingsnorth, there were 1500 mouths to be fed on the final day of action; and during the week, around 800.

Money from neighbourhoods needed to be banked. A team of three coordinators re-ordered food as needed, in conversation with the finance team. The quantity ordered was adjusted as the need arose. It ran strictly to the timetable; the kitchen door shut to the public at other times, so breaks could be taken, and a break for the servers.

Kitchens were volunteer-run but coordinated by experienced cooks on a rota basis. A kitchen with a 250-person capacity would generally require five experienced coordinators (though more would be preferred). The main meal needs around 8 volunteers for chopping as well as washing up help (in two shifts). Bulk stock, lentils and pulses and liquid were added to avoid drying out and burning. Sufficient protein, though, was in my opinion, in short supply.

Food was the big-ticket item for Climate Camp. With a budget of £12,000, it started with a £5000 credit from a wholesaler, and £500 of vegetables and bread (a two-day supply). It was paid back by donations at the camp, the required charge was £28 a week/£4 a day. The surplus achieved, £5000 went towards funding the following camp (in London).

The fundraising group collated funding bids from each working group. It made the following pledges. It would not take money:

1. Which comes with attached conditions which in any way threaten to compromise the aims of the camp or decisions of the organising group from multinational corporations;
2. From organisations which require 'sponsorship' deals;
3. From individuals/organisations, which the group judges are incompatible with camp aims.

In the run-up to the following year's Climate Camp, it took a stall for a 2007 fundraiser at a music festival: *Big Green Gathering*. They put up, a *Last Chance Saloon* bar, that year as a fundraiser for the camp. Bath Brewery supplied the ale. It was held between 1–5 August that year, on a farm near Cheddar Gorge.

The welcome tent was the first visit for newcomers to any camp, new arrivals could pick up a guidebook (*lonely planet*) that described, in graphic form, the way the protest camp worked, the rules, and its horizontal governance structure (see chapter 9). These Climate Camp guidebooks, published for every Climate Camp from 2006 to 2010, were loosely based on the popular, *lonely planet* guides. They became increasingly sophisticated and detailed as time passed. Mark Kennedy helpfully scripted a guide to setting up the camp, and the following section is based on his notes.

At the back of the welcome tent was a site office. This was running more like a builders' merchant. This checked tools out, matching tools to needs if possible, connecting them to a specialist if that's required, or directing them to the welcome/action support/workshop/tent if that's what it turns out they are after, and fobbing them off in the nicest possible way if they're just wasting time. Deliveries may turn up and need to be directed to the person responsible. A reception was a rota job, as you can only do so many hours of answering the same questions over and over again. In later years, the site office was combined.

Camp set-up involves a lot of different bodies as well as self-tooled-up crafts folk, a big supply of tools. Signing in and out of a book is essential. At the 2007 event, many of the activists lent out their own tools for the duration of the event, on trust that they would not be lost. To this end, all the tools and electrical kits that came in were indexed and labelled (in permanent marker, rather than removable stickers). Not all came back.

In terms of power for the camp, a £3000 budget was allocated to generate electricity using carbon-neutral off-grid technology. Just like National Grid, supply always has to exceed demand. Batteries were used to bridge the supply gap, and to store power after dark. Power providers were then matched to power users, to minimise battery movements, encourage cooperation and share responsibility. In the event, none of the August camps suffered from a lack of wind or sun; so backup biodiesel generators were not required. Solar and wind energy were encouraged. Large mobile-solar powered providers brought expensive equipment to a squatted site with a heavy police presence (although only UHF connectors were actually seized).

Neighbourhoods were generally self-sufficient in power, some using wind and sun, their own equipment, but the site-working group linked them up. They were all connected to the grid. At the first camp, it was a single buried spur; at subsequent camps, the main voltage ring main was used. These were placed under boards across roadways so as to avoid trip hazards, or suspended from poles; labelled to avoid accidents. The water supply used the same principle.

Be the Media

Psand.net provided virtual access to the wider world outside the camp, covering the issues being discussed at the workshops, and independently of mobile phone expenses and coverage issues, directly to the satellite. It allowed the campers to upload their stories (usually to the *Indymedia* website), in a direct, participatory and democratic way, and without moderation or editing. There was also a TV studio tent, visionOntv.

This was a fully functioning media centre for use by the campers, powered mainly by a pedal-bike/battery. Five minutes of pedal power was enough for ten minutes of laptop use! I was most impressed with Bristol wireless and the *psand.net* uplink. Slow maybe; speed was a paltry 0.5Mb/sec uplink and 2Mb/sec download. A caravan housed twelve networked laptops, adequate for the purpose.

It is ironic that the Internet was originally invented by, of all people, the US military, as a multi-nodal comms system, before being taken up by universities after HTML was strapped on it. Its release to the whole world has had intended, and not so welcome, consequences. *This has greatly sped up information dissemination for socially networked individuals.* While a Guardian Google hangout or zoom conference may now seem routine, *Skype* and *Twitter* had only just been invented in 2006. We were quite cutting edge at the time in our use of satellite uplink. There was no Instagram or Snapchat then.

The media policy was resented by many journalists, who, like John Vidal, may have felt these new socially networked individuals were usurping their role, and distrust resulted. *Facebook* and *Twitter* were to be in full use, and had, for example, been used extensively to cover the 7/7 bombings in London during the Gleneagles conference.

Climate Camp radio was also broadcasting twice a day on some FM frequency during the camp; each show was between 90 and 120 minutes long. *Dissident Island show* podcasts were available for download after each show and as an RSS feed on the Climate Camp for webcasting. Most of these websites are no longer online. There was even an internet TV station.

The medics were in touch with the local hospital via a hotline when required for medical emergencies. There were two doctors on call at all times, working shifts. They ran the clinic, which opened for 2 hours each day, from their tent. This all proved necessary to isolate dysentery cases and prevent that from spreading. Access was coordinated via the information tent.

The tabloid press had a field day ridiculing the proceedings. The *Daily Mail* had the best copy. Writing about the London neighbourhood, it related that: 'It all feels like the prelude to the Russian Revolution of 1917, but with more colourful clothing, and bigger hair.' In point of fact, the demographic was, from my experience, largely graduate and mostly employed.

The single most difficult task was where to find the site of the camp. This task fell to the land group and closed to anyone else. The insecurity of usually squatted land threatened to undermine security. This would also hinder outreach. Since the general location was dependent on campaign options decided by the rest, the search was put off until a few months before. All sorts of problems could emerge, for instance: Squatting open land accords no legal protection, despite all the legal notice, the landowner could come in or the police could declare the whole thing a trespasser assembly. 'Premises' were squatted which even includes vehicles. The other option discussed, but this was too expensive, was to purchase some land.

Squatting seemed very much in line with the ethos of the camp. Perhaps this was because the core group lived in a co-op. There may be pragmatic (rather than principled) arguments for renting or purchasing. What about Common Land? No, it wouldn't have commoners' rights. Wherever you are, the police will try to contain you on the land where you settle.

Now, however, squatting has become illegal in England and Wales, as the coalition legislated, and it is now a criminal offence to occupy land without consent. (It already was in Scotland, although there is a right to pitch a tent up there).

Justice Minister Crispin Blunt said: 'I am clear that the days of so-called squatters' rights must end and squatters who break the law receive a proper punishment.' Meanwhile, housing minister Grant Shapps would tip 'the scales of justice in favour of the law-abiding homeowner once and for all.'

'The idea that squatters break into people's homes while they are out at the shops is a right-wing media myth. It simply doesn't happen – and one of the reasons why is because squatting in someone's home is already a criminal offence.' Promises that the government would 'remove limits on the rights to peaceful protest', were to be included in the *Protection of Freedoms bill,* (which was supposed to have been the vehicle for this reform). It never was. So 'aggravated trespass' remains on the statute book.

The construction site evolved into a co-op with an undercover director! *The Activist Tat Collective*: Mark Stone (aka Kennedy) the undercover cop, got himself appointed director of the collective for administrative purposes. This loaned out everything from tools to compost toilets. According to collective member Belinda Day, 'We started out just getting stuff together for Climate Camp but we now have loads of tat. We've had to put together a database to keep track of everything. We have plumbing stuff, cooking utensils, electrical equipment, compost toilets, and communication equipment (walkie-talkies).'

This 'Tat' was widely hired out internationally; to a peace camp, an animal rights gathering, Radical Roots, Earth First, Sheffield Bike Festival and numerous other events. Some even went to France, to *No Borders* camp in Calais. Apparently, much of this equipment is still in a lock-up, literally mothballed; whose whereabouts are known only to Kennedy.

Hired or paid in advance were vehicles, fuel costs and insurance to cover and drivers. It fell to the available van owners, like Mark Kennedy, to manage and store the tat, apparently using his government credit card! The toilets were prefabricated from pallets and straw bales, familiar to anybody who has attended any festivals. Three hundred small bales of straw would be required for a 1,200 people site.

Contracts were drawn up with local farmers to buy back the resulting manure, stored in wheelie bins. Vegetables and straw came from these farms, timber, soaking materials such as straw. Pallets and timber were sourced from sawmills, who always need to offload ply off-cuts and sawdust. Storage space then had to be found in advance. Later on, a lock-up was hired. Sink tops consisted of an ordinary 'sit-on' stainless steel sink and stand, supported on timber from old pallets, and located next to toilets and kitchens. On-site, the gate was manned 24/7. The mediation team liaised. Volunteers from the neighbourhoods, or 'barrios', were roped in to clean toilets. Barrios were bounded by oil barrels, filled with water, framing the fire lanes. The barrels were filled with the first issue, of around 500 gallons, off the hydrant, to flush the rust from the hydrant main. Hand-washes using bowls and buckets were put in before running water was supplied by the water group. The toilets were prefabricated off-site, from plywood and pallets. Urine and faeces were kept separate. If you collect urine separately in containers to soak, it reduces quantity drastically. Unlike faeces, urine is actually a sterile liquid and can be retained in straw bales, which makes it an excellent compost. This can happen on or off-site, (although it became increasingly less pleasant to handle).

Environmental Health would then be contacted to test the water. Nevertheless, dysentery did set in at the first camp, boiling the water was advisable since it was not regular drinking water.

Outstanding issues were ironed out at site-wide meetings. A typical start to the day for neighbourhoods was a breakfast meeting, prior to the main site ones. These were not centrally managed. Housekeeping Issues arising out of camp policy were discussed, such as whether to accept the police's latest ultimatum. Decisions are eventually reached via consensus, and 'spokes' are delegated to express the collective's views to the 'spokes council', before reporting back. This can seem like a long-winded process if you're used to giving/taking orders, but it did ensure that everyone had ownership over decisions, and are usually happy to implement them. All societies have their warriors, farmers, artisans, artists, and groups of every sort. Being open to and welcoming diversity is what makes a society responsive and resilient.

Each neighbourhood and group would then send a spoke/representative to the main site. Observers were allowed, but only spokes and facilitators could speak – that was intended to make the meetings more manageable. When they ran smoothly, it could all be done in no more than an hour. When there were too many issues, it rambled on, as it exceeded group attention span.

Following the first planning meeting, the camp steering group met monthly around the country, either at social centres or in squats. Policies were formulated at interminable weekend meetings. I still remember it took *five* hours, one cold February Sunday afternoon, in Nottingham (Sumac centre) to reach an agreement about the addition of the word 'non-violent' in the phrase 'direct action'. This is the Delphi decision-making process in action, as we will see in Chapter 9.

Those held in Shoreditch ('Rampart squat') were also photographed by the Forward Intelligence Team (or *FIT squad*).

Around 150 people were involved. There were seventeen working groups included Wellbeing, Kids, Welcome & Tranquillity, Medics, Workshops, Land group, Legal, Defence, Gate, Action Support, Outreach and Media, Website, International, Action training, Process and Finance. Some of these were working behind the scenes for an hour a week or less, others were doing it more like a part-time job for several months. Some worked on the camp for over 8 months, others did their bit nearer the start or end of the process. At each monthly weekend-long gathering (where key decisions were agreed) there were between 40-80 people. Some people came to every gathering, some to most, and some just to one. So there was a core of the same people (maybe 30) every time, but the group might be different every time.

I went to almost all the monthly organising meetings, missing just two. I did come across some of the yet-to-be-found out undercover cops, but they blended in only too well. 'Anyone can be trained and become part of a working group – if you're interested in the media, you join the media working group, and then you go to smaller consensus meetings, where people who cannot be bothered with the press releases and keep sending them out'. These were smaller groups with a specific focus, e.g. networking (website, media and publicising the camp) and Site Practicalities (infrastructure and transport). They had the autonomy to work on their particular areas, but if any decisions would affect the whole process or camp, they had to be taken to the full gathering, and decided by everyone, using the Delphi method (see Chapter 9).

Because of all this meticulous pre-planning, there appeared to be no obvious management on-site; this was perceived as something of a miracle by visiting journalists and visitors alike. The campers had elected to fill roles as required '...whether they wished to prepare food, design posters, sing songs, stage presentations about their views on environmental issues or organise a group of like-minded protesters to go and form an instant human barrier on a terminal access road'. Though this seemed a good idea at the time, 'solidarity and identity are most effectively created under conditions of threat', this *modus operandi* was lost to newcomers.

Transport was a big-ticket item. It involved both vehicles and phones. A driver shortage limited what could be provided. The driver is the person responsible for his vehicle at the time if it is stopped. The driver had to take responsibility for his vehicle.

A shuttle service, using a bio-fuel powered diesel bus, was the responsibility of the transport team. This had to be run as a free service because it would be illegal to charge under the law (public service vehicle regulations), a license fee is required. The police regarded this as an 'illegal taxi service'.

Phone trees were useful. These are basically networks in which a phone call triggers a cascade of pre-arranged numbers, and so on until everyone has got the message. This is the easiest and cheapest way to spread messages quickly down the line. This could be an emergency alert (such as the start of work or an eviction) or just a regular means of dissemination, without having to ring everyone individually!

One tree was reserved for emergencies; the other broadcast recorded information; a public phone number was used to book bus places from the transport tent. That number is linked to mobile in each of the shuttle buses. Groups that helped during the camp – such as medics, prisoner support or legal observers used the tree.

Daily meetings held each morning in each *barrio* were concerned with routine housekeeping (such as cooking and washing up rotas, night-time noise in the camping area, rubbish handling, and socials).

The climate campers decided to restrict police liaisons to just two people. One would have sufficed but it was believed the police might attempt to play one person off against another. When the camp started, they could call on emergency support from a standby group, consisting of representatives from each neighbourhood and also key working groups, to reach quick decisions. These *buddies*, if faced with a potential emergency situation, could call an emergency mini-spokes-council and mediation team. This solution cut the corner when full consensus decision-making would have been too slow.

The Camp legal team was kept busy dealing with 'stop and search' orders, recruiting, training; equipping and coordinating legal observers to support activists during actions. They gathered evidence for use in subsequent legal cases and liaised with the police after arrests.

'Legal observation and police monitoring…can make a real difference from collating the data necessary for effective legal challenges, to providing and collecting witness statements for those arrested. These actions have both challenged the way protest and the streets are policed and kept innocent people out of prison.' They also provided an *arrestee support phone line* to track those arrested during Climate Camp actions outside. The group continued to expose the police strategy long after the camp.

The premise behind all camp workshops was to explore each and every solution to climate change, rather than seek international agreement 'A large problem like global warming does not necessarily need to be dealt with by a large solution; we can begin to tackle it with small solutions inside a large framework'. Implementation was 'bottom up'. The finance group had to juggle the available kitty among the different groups, by means of budget bids. There were also smaller working groups (e.g. entertainments, kids) who worked more through phone calls and e-mail. Working groups did lots of work outside of gatherings and many met between gatherings.

I heard that the finance group was particularly under strength, so I joined that; not that I had any experience in that field. On-site, I decided to run a workshop on eco-architecture and joined the tranquillity team.

Chapter 8

The Gleneagles G8 the Prequel

The Climate Camp for Action had its roots; one could almost say its dress rehearsal, in the mobilisation against the G8 meeting that was held at Gleneagles in 2005. This was a whole year prior to the first camp at Drax.

The 'Horizon' camp in Stirling housed the majority of people who took action against the G8. It was some 15 miles from the village of Auchterarder, where the hotel was situated. Between 2500 and 5000 attended that camp. Over the previous two years, several attempts had been made to find farmland close to Gleneagles for the eco-village. These had failed.

Two significant networks emerged to contest the 2005 G8 Gleneagles Summit. *Make Poverty History* was the largest of the three networks which, at its peak, consisted of a membership of over 500 British and Irish NGOs, religious groups and high-profile celebrities. Many of these had previously been involved with the Jubilee in Birmingham, a symbolic celebration of forgiveness of debt. G8 '*Alternatives*' was a smaller and largely Scottish network of trade unions, political parties, NGOs and academics. Its key event was a marshalled march past the fence of the

Gleneagles Hotel on 6 July 2005, the first day of the G8 Summit, attended by over 10,000 people. This was the group I managed to join.

Back in Sterling, police put up a security cordon around the entrance on Thursday morning (6 July) at 2.30 am. Roads around Stirling had also been closed to prevent a repeat of Wednesday's rioting in the town. Central Police Scotland said it took this action after protesters had poured out of the camp and ran amok in and around Stirling on Wednesday. In both locations, and in between, blockades were set up on road and rail links, largely by campers from Stirling. Sir Bob Geldof (as the self-appointed leader of *Make Poverty History*) labelled the road blockaders 'thugs'. Meanwhile, back in Edinburgh, loads of white *Make Poverty History* T-shirts and fashionable white armbands were sold.

Gleneagles was within striking distance of Stirling (about 15 miles away), which was just across the Ochil Hills from the camp. Stirling Council had offered an old landfill site in a loop of river meadow, overlooking the Wallace Monument and the hills. Senior police sources were critical of the Council for allowing protesters to camp there in the first place. Unbeknown to them, it was Mark Kennedy, with the presumed approval of his supervisor, who had suggested this site, as he revealed in 2011: It was in an oxbow in the river, constraining the egress of its participants to the town side. With only one entrance, the chosen site should have been easy for the police to blockade. Not that it was ideal.

Undercover man Mark Kennedy (aka Mark Stone) earned him the title 'Transport Mark'. He was one of the prime organisers, moving people and equipment to and from the protest base camp. The red and black flag of social anarchism and the rebel skull and crossbones of piracy flew over the entrance. The Wallace monument, the ultimate symbol of Scottish independence, stood emblematically on an escarpment opposite. Part of this campsite was an old landfill that gave off methane, so smoking had to be banned. It was split into zones or barrios which brought their own catering facilities. The *Common Place* in Leeds bought their furniture (its sinks, cinema, chairs and books) up to Scotland.

This organisational stamp was then used for the three following "Climate Camps" massed protests against power stations and airports in Drax, Kingsnorth and Heathrow. Police claimed, '…it provided 200 to 300 violent anarchists with a base from which to attack the summit. *Dissent!* Activists certainly saw it as a "political opportunity".'

The Stirling camp pioneered many of the features used at subsequent ones. Take the early warning system, for example. To prevent the police from launching any surprise night raids on the camp, 20-30 volunteers manned the gate 24/7 at any one time for nearly a week while surrounded by riot police. They would often spend hours literally face to face across a 3-feet high farm fence with FIT teams/dog handlers. They made the whole 'no police on site' thing a reality.

To avoid entrapment, affinity groups had begun leaving the site around twelve hours before the start of the summit and before lockdown, hiding in the forests and suburbs along the way to Gleneagles. This allowed them to spring into action as the delegates arrived by car in the morning. These hard-core groups blockaded many roads around Gleneagles that morning. Some *Dissent* members even claimed they had left posing as pantomime cows – to escape possible detection by helicopters using night-vision (infrared) photography.

As darkness fell, many in the eco-village had scattered into the hills and forests around Gleneagles. By the time the police realised what was happening, it was too late. Tree trunks, rocks, branches were being laid across the M9 in the early hours. As the Green Party spokes said, the camp was subject to continued attack throughout the weeks it was based there. The chair of the Green party, barrister Hugo Charlton, commented on the substantial mistreatment of prisoners by Scottish police.

He went on to say: 'More seriously, despite the substantial police presence and preparation, detainees have been held in unacceptable conditions. (They) were made to wait in a police van, with their hands handcuffed behind their backs for 11 hours at Falkirk police station with little water and not allowed to go to the toilet. One female detainee was obliged to urinate in the van.'

Superintendent Gavin Buist said there were a minority of troublemakers at the camp, but stressed most were 'passionate, committed protesters' with no interest in disruptive behaviour. Matt Sellwood, of the Oxford Green party, commented: 'Police behaviour here amounts to a serious attempt to repress and crush legitimate protesters. The methods used have clearly broken the law and the principle of transparent justice. Only today I have been cordoned into my camp (twice) and cordoned outside (once). No reason other than preventing peaceful protests was given, and the police gave no justification in law.'

The remaining 250 camp activists met to determine whether or not to have a large mass march Plan (the 'suicide' march) leave the camp. It was led by a bodhran player. Historically used in battles and parades, this is the traditional Celtic drum. On this occasion, it was accompanied by a didgeridoo. They marched the five miles to the M9 motorway. Hundreds of riot police attempted to kettle them. This precipitated the violence. The whole thing then turned a bit like 'Braveheart' violent. Supermarket trolleys were filled with cobblestones and fought their way out. In one of its more creative incidents, they used poisonous Hogwarts flowers that caused huge welts and blisters on the police.

After five minutes, the police lines were pushed back fifty feet, opening a small path through to a suburban residential area. Many were able to push through the kettle. Most of the rest were separated into various police lines to disappear into fields or return to camp. (From the former *Dissent* website)

Meanwhile, back in Edinburgh, I was based in a friend's flat in Edinburgh throughout that week. I was able to actually travel by train and coach to get to Gleneagles. The first coaches did not get through, because of disorder on the M8. Buses eventually left at 2.30 pm – two hours later than scheduled. It later transpired that it was only the rumour about a march on the US Embassy in Edinburgh that had swung our way. Our coach was stopped on the way by police, but we got there eventually. There was a planned route, but many left that to cross a field towards the huge steel barrier surrounding the hotel. Riot police were flown in by Chinook helicopter.

These tactics had reduced the numbers to a more manageable 500 or so. *Make Poverty History* had been on the streets all week. Their two peaceful demonstrations took place on 2 July and 5 July (the same day as the Gleneagles demonstration). These started up in Edinburgh at around 10.30 AM, as coach-loads of protesters prepared to depart for Gleneagles. The atmosphere was good-humoured until the police announced that the march had been cancelled at 12 AM. This was because of the chaos on the A9 road at Stirling caused by the campers. The Black Bloc anarchists were already occupying motorway flyovers on either side of Auchterarder.

With 1,500 people on the streets in Edinburgh, the police needed to get as many away to Auchterarder as possible, to avoid a blockade of the American embassy. Demonstrators blew whistles on top of bus stops in Princes Street and flew black flags. Missiles were thrown and arrests were made.

Auchterarder residents were issued with security passes to go about their business, as much of their village was cordoned off with security fencing. It was virtually deserted, as many residents had decided to leave for the duration. The perimeter fence split the Northwestern perimeter of the village and the hotel conference centre. Everyone else was subject to stop-and-search. The police were using $60 of the *Prevention of Terrorism* Act to stop, search, photograph and demand proof of identity from anyone travelling through the area. The government had also signed a blanket exception to Freedom of Information legislation for all matters relating to the summit.

The outcome of these talks was a disappointment to all concerned; particularly to the delegates. As the protests and repression were taking place, a summit to deliver Africa into the arms of the G8's corporations and abandon the (already heavily compromised) Kyoto treaty climate change, at

Gleneagles Hotel behind the fences and armed police. It seemed to be more about opening new markets and applying economic dependency; a mere step away from outright control.

But much worse was to follow the 7/7 London Bombing, the next day came as a complete shock. Days later, the camp was taken down. It even brought the G8 to a halt; the police returned to London in force. (See Chapter 14)

Despite the need felt by many activists to keep their actions in check, the reality was that there was a little protest planned for 7 July. A memorial in solidarity with, and in memory of, victims of the London bombings were erected in the camp. It was all over.

On 8 July, police organised a free train from Stirling to London, in a further effort to clear the camp. It was estimated there were as many as 250,000 protesters, all in Scotland. Stirling's *horizon* prototype was the prototype adopted for the Climate Camp, along with the neighbourhood model and consensus decision-making process. The following year, we were told that the original 'leaders' had dropped out. This turned out to be untrue, the undercover cop Kennedy continued.

The point of protest is maximum publicity, maximum disruption, minimal damage, no injuries, and the minimisation of the arrest. These issues would be foremost in any style of protest from then on.

Chapter 9

The Horizontal Organisation
Consensus and Affinity

Consensus decision-making is currently integral to direct action; participation rather than a representation of the top-down hierarchy. You're the total of whatever you get up to.

Rejection of hierarchy, exploitation and oppression may be empowering but it is uncomfortable; without authority. The inhuman part of it, the ability to keep one's distance as a spectator and to rise above things, is ultimately...human. 'What does it really matter?' Is a line we like to associate with bourgeois callousness, but it is the line most likely to make the individual aware, without dread, of the '...insignificance of his/ her existence.'

This consensus model is known as the *Delphi technique.* It was pioneered in the UK by the Quakers. It was later formalised by academics and in industry. *Seeds for change* is the leading NGO advocacy group for this movement in the UK, and we followed their method with slavish adherence. The three-step process for achieving 'Oneness of mind' involves:

1. Setting a *thesis*.
2. Considering the *antithesis*.
3. And then proceeding to the *synthesis*.

It is the method of choice for the internet/mobile generation. It has also been adopted by academics. It requires a common cause: because it would not be rational to take part in an ineffective group, and consensus decisions need active co-operation. It contributes to community 'ownership', or thesis resolution. It also works against a bully trying to swing a particular course of action. Consensus works something like this: Introduce a proposal, then:

- Gather initial thoughts and reactions.
- List issues and concerns?
- Collecting ideas and proposals for solutions and writing them down – the antithesis.
- Discussing the ideas – What are the pros and cons?

Consensus is a creative thinking process that thrives on a *mash-up*. Make time for a broad-ranging discussion, where you can explore ideas and look at the pros and cons. This will often spark new and surprising ideas. Reservations need to be brought up early on so that they can be dealt with as a friendly amendment. This is the *antithesis*. Modify some proposals, eliminate others and develop a shortlist of favourites. Look for a way to bring together the best qualities of the remaining ideas.

A proposal is then put forward out of the ideas that are left. This is the *synthesis*. Discuss the pros and cons of the proposal – make sure everybody has a chance to contribute. Are there any friendly amendments to the proposal that make it more acceptable to the group? Test for agreement: Are there any major objections that you can't overcome? Acknowledge minor objections. Check for agreement: Is there a consensus? Are there friendly amendments? Decision agreed. People own their tasks.

The agreed hand signals are intended to preclude rude interruptions, they were used at the main camp too, both within each group and among all groups together. For the facilitator, these cue their feedback:

Active agreement – consciously participating in a decision and showing agreement using the 'jazzy' hands signal. If not, then think whether the idea needs to be re-formulated;

One voice at a time – avoiding discussion drifting off-topic and hope participants can use hand signals to correct this;

Hand signals to be taught at the beginning of the session:

- ✓ 1 finger raised – 'I would like to speak.'
- ✓ 2 fingers raised – I've got something immediately relevant to say.'
- ✓ 'Jazz hands' – 'I support the idea currently being discussed.'
- ✓ Fist–I block this proposal. A 'block' kills a proposal: a total veto. Everyone may have the right to block. In normal consensus, people normally block for two reasons – 1) A proposal will split the group OR 2) The group is failing to make a decision. If a new proposal is blocked then, this flags the need for a new

decision. In an ideal world, have a counter-proposal ready before you can block a proposal.

✓ A stand-aside – a disagreement over consent. This allows the proposal (whatever it is) to go ahead in the name of the group. Those that stand aside, however, will take no part in that action. Too many of these and the process itself will self-destruct.

✓ *Temperature Checks* were used as an ongoing indicator – people were either asked to stand in the part of the room that best represented their opinion in response to the current scenario or to signify by use of their fingers.

✓ Five fingers for strong support and a willingness to lead the proposal forward.

✓ Four fingers for strong support, and a willingness to work on it.

✓ Three fingers for minimal support, but a willingness to work for it.

✓ Two fingers for neutrality.

✓ One finger for no support.

✓ Fist for no support and active opposition.

Because it would not be rational to take part in an ineffective group, a consensus decision-making process encourages active co-operation; but it cannot work unless there is a common cause; that cause was the camp. The clever psychology of Delphi was that it let activists feel they owned their input. It felt unfamiliar for newcomers, but it was easier for the working groups because they were familiar with the process and they understood the purpose.

The ideal outcome would be the 'friendly amendment'. This allows the debate to move forward, with a concern for improving an existing idea and making it more effective.

If there are significant reservations, the group may amend or reword the proposal. The signals are used to propel the process, but they can be very slow. My own experience of planning meetings was that it was worth it at the main event. It was a hot summer Saturday. I remember a squatted school, (St Ethelred's) within sight of Canary wharf; Ian Pei's pyramid office block on the skyline, and a visit to an 'Art not Oil' exhibition in Dalston.

The truth is, the further away from consensus, the more wearisome it is. This tended to happen at main camp meetings. There is always the danger that a compromise will drive the group toward their least preferred option. On the plus side, it does deal effectively with the problem of bullying. You are willing to let the proposal pass but want to register your concerns. You may even put energy into implementing the idea once your dissent has been acknowledged. If consensus building could eliminate conflict, save time, and always lead to better policy, enthusiasm for it would be better deserved.

Affinity groups, by contrast, were based on a different model; the Zapatista model we looked at in chapter 2. These autonomous small groups were organised in a non-hierarchical and self-sufficient way. The Groups shared their hopes (outcomes), fears, experiences, strengths and weaknesses. They agree on the form of the action in advance. For a group to work, everyone must follow their agreed role, which should dovetail with the other members of the group, even in stressful situations. Scenarios likely to be encountered are discussed (for example, police intervention or violence). These are coordinated by mobile phones and/or Twitter.

In this view, people so empowered go further and try harder than those who feel under peer group pressure. 'Real' protests with 'real' meaning could interfere with the processes of global forces. Anarchism, the relationship between individuals, sits uneasily with consensus-decision-making: '...after a while, seeking consensus became tortured, a time-waster, and its reason for being the only decision-making approach became steadily less compelling.' The site meetings had become longer, as this blogger notes:

The principle of 'stand aside' was meant to deal with these difficulties. The problem is that a biased facilitator could still steer a group to make the decisions he or she wants to see happen.

The Camp's great strength was that theory and practice in a shared space for a week every year. In 2010, it had disintegrated to the extent that one camper could write:

'I don't think anyone wanted this outcome at Climate Camp, but the fact is because things were not always done in a collective way, it could be pretty alienating for new people like me. *Whereas in the early years the core had the plan in their heads, a large number of people didn't know what was going on in later years.* Those who did have strong affinity groups and experience didn't plan for mass action at the site, peeled off to do small fringe actions in town, against the offices of energy companies or the RBS sponsored Fringe festival.'

In the real world, oligarchies are the normal.' So wrote German syndicalist sociologist Robert Michaels in his 1911 book, *Political Parties*. It has happened in all forms of organisation, regardless of how democratic or autocratic they may be at the start. The reasons behind that process are: 'the indispensability of leadership; the tendency of all groups, including the organisation leadership, to defend their interests; the *passivity of the led individuals* more often than not taking the form of actual gratitude towards the leaders.'

Any attempt to run a country by the Delphi method, I believe, would be doomed to failure, but horses for courses, this was adopted at the camp as a 'fait-accompli'. While it had worked adequately in the run-up to the first camp, it was cumbersome in later years, culminating in its eventual irrelevance. This was when the block was imposed without an alternative (no. 7 on the list).

Chapter 10

Drax – The First Climate Camp (24 August – 4 September 2006)

One of the biggest successes of 2007 was the way the camp movement re-invigorated the green movement. I believe the camp broke down these fears and directly contributed to Climate Change legislation. Climate campaigning has always been a daunting task: Where do you start? Where can you really have an effect?

After six monthly campaign meetings, the first target was picked – whittled down from a shortlist of three. Drax power station was located in the so-called 'Megawatt' valley in Yorkshire. This was so-called because it was home to a number of large coal-fired power stations. The second-highest vote called for the occupation of the A14/M6 motorway junction in Northamptonshire. Drax was chosen in 2006 on the basis that it was the single largest carbon dioxide emitter in Western Europe (8% of UK electric output) and had a maximum potential consumption of 36,000 tonnes of coal a day – and 20 million tonnes output of CO^2 per year at that time.

Four hundred rendezvoused at Selby railway station with the intention of occupying a field outside the town. They were led to the chosen site by the Land group. It was sheep pasture and very rural, located about 3km from the power station itself, flat and well-drained pasture. Next door was the Barlow Common Nature Reserve. The 'inner' land group had negotiated a week lease from a local farmer.

'On behalf of the staff at Barlow Common Nature Reserve, we would like to express our thanks and gratitude for the efficiency and managerial aptitude displayed during your recent encampment. There was no mess, litter or damage found on the reserve attributable to the campers which in itself reflects the high standards you set out to attain. Many of the campers we met were friendly, genuine, and committed people. There is a markedly strong affinity between the reserve staff and yourselves over environmental issues and we believe you made your point...'

The final site plan was agreed upon in the last monthly meeting before the start of June. A big map was covered in stickies, and a setup timeline was agreed – with jobs written on post-it notes and labelled with the names of willing volunteers.

The site coordinator marked out the ground plan for the camp. The fire lanes and public structures, such as the central kitchen, first toilet block, site office, and regional barrios, were defined. The water team connected the ring main. Neighbourhoods laid out their own areas. Also, the initial set-up on-site (known as the 'swoop'), was always very vulnerable and a quick, smooth, set-up helped with this. Luckily, the weather was excellent. It also helped charge up the battery bank for the night.

Not all-camp gossip was helpful to the cause. Inconsiderate talk by some campers put off many locals (many of whom worked at the power stations). This ill-feeling came to a head later that week, after an unpleasant incident with a local tractor driver. This was picked up by regional media: the *Yorkshire Post* described the campers as '...a malign influence on the debate over future power supplies, with the result that we'll soon be facing regular power cuts'.

Drax was the largest carbon-emitter in Europe, more than even Heathrow. At that time, it was generating around 7% of the country's electricity, about 4GW. 'Workers at the plant were bemused by the protest. Drax, they said, was the cleanest and most efficient coal-fired power station in the UK, complete with the best scrubbing technology to remove sulphur dioxide. It emitted less CO_2 per unit of electricity produced than other coal stations in the UK. Why were the less efficient generators not the target, they wondered?' No coal went into Drax that day, with the railway line being blocked off by protesters. Internal coalbunkersc within the plant had a big enough capacity to keep the station running at capacity for 60 hours without external supply, so there was no chance that disruption could be more than symbolic.

The local police chief, Deputy Chief Constable Ian McPherson, took a more measured view: 'The majority (has) impressed us as sincere, responsible people...what is concerning the police is the group of anarchists at the core of the protest. Many of these are veterans of violent May Day protests, the anti-globalisation riots in Seattle and the British anti-road protests of the 1990s'.

The issue of hard-core campers continued to be a concern for the police throughout and was to come to a head two years later at another power station protest in Kent (Kingsnorth). Drax Power Ltd, for their part, were granted an injunction in connection with the camp, prohibiting trespass on the power station site…and restricting the use of a footpath along the site boundary.

Drax (as of 2019) is half coal-fired, has three of its six modules burning imported wood pellets. A spokesperson said: 'Biomass is typically *three to five times* more expensive than coal, once all factors are considered, and we cannot embark upon a major investment scheme without confidence in the future of the Renewables Obligation (RO) and the market it enables'.

Drax relies on this subsidy to reduce its coal consumption. Both coal and biomass are imported and that generates pollution and carbon emissions. Woodchip is shipped all the way across the Atlantic from *North Carolina,* at great expense. Whether it has saved that much CO^2 is questionable. Almost 800 scientists wrote to the EU government last year to call for biomass to be stripped of its carbon-neutral status. This had not gone unnoticed in America. As one Carolina academic noted: 'But here's the bigger picture, the thing that astounds my friends who had no idea this "sustainability" perversion is going on: the only reason why cutting our forests meets the EU standard for greenhouse gas emissions is because emissions are measured only at your power plants.'

What was missing then from the equation were the effects of the carbon sequestration, lost as trees are cut down, or the carbon that is emitted by the massive pellet-chipping plants, the carbon spewed from smog-emitting logging and pellet trucks, or the emissions from the ships that transport our timber pellets across the Atlantic to UK power plants.

'This configuration of replacing lost carbon through unnatural supplementation (fertilisers) disturbs the delicate balance of the Earth's carbon cycle. As a result, more carbon is released into the atmosphere, leaving the soil unable to reabsorb extra outputs and cumulative overall greenhouse gas emissions.'

How can we increase the carbon content of soil? Through 'regenerative' farming practices, says Perry, including planting cover crops, no-till farming, rotating crops, reducing chemicals and fertilisers, and managed grazing (combining trees, forage plants and livestock together in an integrated system, a technique called 'silvopasture'). These practices have been demonstrated to sequester carbon into the soil and keep it there, resulting in carbon-enriched soils that are healthier and more resilient to extreme weather conditions with improved water permeability, preventing the rainwater runoff that contributes to rising sea levels and rising temperatures. Of the carbon that is found in soils—which, remarkably, amounts to more than the amount of carbon found in plants and the atmosphere combined—a substantial proportion is bound up in tough organic compounds produced by fungi. Cropland soil amendment trials using basalt rock dust and compost amendments on greenhouse gas emissions from the soil have the potential to capture carbon and improve crop yields, and plant and microbial health. Not till agriculture, involving seed drilling instead of ploughing, is another lower-carbon alternative for some crops.

Materials for the site were fabricated at Leeds Common Place, a social centre, which hosted many community groups, Activists there had previous experience from Stirling the previous year. Large reels of plastic pipe were connected up to a fire hydrant just outside the site (and inconveniently laid across a country lane). Much of the material used to create structures for the camp was reclaimed waste. It was scavenged from building sites and would otherwise have been sent to landfill – such as pallets, timber off-cuts, plywood. Compost toilets, comprehensive recycling, grey water systems and a pedal-powered laundry were in use at Drax. All food was vegan, mostly organic. It was provided by the communal neighbourhood kitchens, many associated with the Social Centres Network (Brighton, Oxford, Nottingham, Manchester and Leeds). Undercover clown 'Lynn Watson', was the founding trustee!

Social Centres hosted events like meetings, gigs, cinema, workshops, language classes, open access computers, talks, film and 'zine-making festivals', free schools, shops, action planning, national gatherings, cooking courses, skill shares and self-defence classes.

There were a number of solar panels and a mains spur to the stage though the electricity distribution grid would wait for subsequent years. 2kW of renewable energy generated that year – equal amounts of solar and wind, plus pedal-power as required. *Indymedia* ran the media tent and the cinema. We even had a bottle bar. A substantial charge was built up during the day on the solar-powered tractor – battery bank, which powered entertainment in the marquee in the evening. One friend of mine ran the kids tent; another was the resident clown. *Indymedia* had an internet up-link via a satellite, a large dish sitting on some straw bales and pointing towards some distant geo-stationary satellite hundreds of miles away over the equator. All expensive equipment was at risk of confiscation. *Bristol Wireless* ran a network of old laptops, (running open-source Linux), provided by Bristol media. It all ran on 400 watts!

A particular problem was the *water supply*. Not knowing where the site was to be set up meant approaching multiple council hydrant teams in advance and making them aware their services might be called on at short notice. All forms obtained were filled in ahead of time, leaving the location blank, and guessing at the consumption (being cautious so they wouldn't be panicked) and putting usage as washing up and personal washing only (to avoid awkward questions).

As soon as the site was chosen, a small deposit (£150) was paid for an un-metred fire hydrant connection. Contact details/mobile numbers of a person in each office were obtained so that onsite at a weekend, all that had to be done was to ring the correct one and tell them where the camp was, where the nearest hydrant was, and negotiate.

The camp also had a qualified plumber, water authority approved and able to self-certify his work as a supervisor. He had to comply with the *Water Use Regulations 1999;* the principal aim of which was to prevent waste, or any contamination, from getting back into the mains supply. This could easily be achieved using double-check valves.

Fire lanes defined neighbourhood camping areas and taped these off, with oil drums filled with water – the first 500-gallon run-off from the hydrant to clean the pipe. Environmental Health came out to test water quality. Unfortunately, we still had some dysentery, so I am not sure that all water was boiled, as had been advised, but I don't remember it spread, thanks to those precautions.

While it didn't all run completely smoothly – it ran well enough. It took about £30,000 to run the camp, but some of this ironically turned out to be government money, such as the van run by Mark Kennedy. Donations were requested, suggested range: kids free, teenagers £5–10, adult on benefit £10–15, low-waged adult £15–20, above-average wage £25–30. 'If you need to bring a dog, you must register in advance with the facilitation group.' Dogs can become aggressive in unfamiliar crowds. There was a central tools store (but I'm not sure many people knew where it was). Tools kept missing and turning up randomly at different points around the site.

Communications ('comms') had brought half-a-dozen walkie-talkies. These were used to communicate with a car park, which was off site at Selby. Tranquillity team was the eyes and ears of the site, and I was pleased to join it. Later in the week, there was some concern that the ones we had used had been jammed by the police, but it turned out that someone had their finger on the 'send' button. We did not use actual names; instead of aliases like *Tango 1*, etc. One of the main concerns was the car park, which was off site, in an adjacent field opposite the site entrance. It was behind the police lines a 24 hours per day job.

The tranquillity team helped newcomers to settle in and monitored site safety. This was a stewarding role, responsible both for conflict resolution on-site and for manning the gate. The welcome and tranquillity group's decisions were made using discussion and consensus. I was trained for the tranquillity team. With the walkie-talkies issued to us, we patrolled the site – in the most ridiculous pink Stetsons. Can a bloke wearing a pink hat be taken seriously?

For the kids, a crèche was provided with a resident clown (*Kristoff* the clown) who performed a show for the kids, all in their own tent. Very memorably at this camp, Kristoff also made a sausage dog out of balloons, one of which he gave to a policewoman, lacking a dog of her own. You can get away with almost anything as a clown! Also present among the campers were the 'Rebel insurgent clown army' effectively the camp court jesters. 'Rebel clowning is a form of radical political activism that merges non-violent direct action with the ancient art of clowning.' Straight from Kafka, the police *also* had their undercover clown in place, 'Lynn Watson', who was also a trustee of Leeds *Commonplace*.

Well-being and trauma provided massage, quiet space, and generally care for people. The police were stopping and searching all and sundry at our only entry to the site, ostensibly citing $60 of the *Criminal Justice Act*. They even confiscated the toilet-emptying rota on my exit from the site. Mark 'Kennedy' and 'Lynn Watson' were a constant, keeping police fully informed of events. Mark had buried wire cutters at specific points known both to himself and the police, thus preventing any incursion through the perimeter fence. This was an attempt at entrapment, which never materialised.

The limited access by the media was a source of resentment. Journalists had to ask permission to attend meetings from participants, and gain consent for photography, and promise not to disrupt or intrude on any activity that was going on. Journalists were also being harassed by the police in a particularly counterproductive manner.

They were allowed for just an hour each day (11 am, midday) and shadowed by members of the media team. The *Be the media* team were concerned to make sure events were accurately reported, and not misrepresented by editors. They were however particularly important that year as there was no local protest group to raise our profile, (whereas the next year we had at least three pressure groups preparing the way).

The camp team preferred to publish its own photographs. Two resident camp photographers ensured that the camp was well documented for the week in which it ran. Paparazzi could only take photos between 11 am and 1 pm. This particularly upset the environmental editor of the Guardian, John Vidal. He wrote: 'Via its media strategy it threatens to become one more totalitarian, an exclusive group that is neither liked nor taken seriously.'

Three 'favoured' journals would be allowed extended access to the site, up to a maximum of two days and two nights, to end by Friday (before the day of action). These 'chosen ones' would inform the print press or radio, but not TV. They were chosen to have a proven track record of good coverage of social issues, preferably of protests/campaigns, and to deliver a clear outline of what they intended to produce. They would be pre-vetted beforehand. They would have to sign a declaration saying they would not 'publish lies' about the camp. They would then be required to stay in neighbourhoods, encouraged to participate in camp life like any other participant. The journalists would be asked to wear their press pass at all times and to identify themselves as a journalist, all very valiant but unenforceable.

Workshops ran for four days and culminated in the 'day of action'; on Saturday someone climbed a lighting tower, but the fence itself was not breached. Mark did however get into a scuffle with police at the perimeter fence. This enhanced his credibility but wounded him badly. This apparently led to a disciplinary warning for Mark, but it would be many years before it would come to light that he had planted wire cutters at that point!

By the following year, journalists rebelled. The *London Evening Standard* went undercover and, as feared, made up their own fake news (see Heathrow, Chapter 11). The original policy then seemed to have been justified, and another result of the successful consensus decision-making process by 'Be the media' group. By the following year (Kingsnorth) six journalists were encouraged to co-exist. There were no winners here. The irony was, had the mainstream press ignored the Climate Camp, it would have achieved nothing. We got the first three pages of the *Independent!* They also started to make their own cartoons.

Spin-off groups reached secondary targets. A second power station became a target – Hartlepool nuclear power station. One again organised by undercover spy Mark Kennedy! London Rising Tide targeted the offices of *Tulchan Communications,* the PR firm representing Drax Group plc.

The police were concerned. In years they would ramp up their response.

Chapter 11

The Educational Outcome – The Workshops

'The workshops can be thought of as a massive think tank where people could explore radical ideas on how to create an alternative society when climate change had completely and irrevocably demolished the mass consumerist lifestyle.' This aim, education, was one of the founding principles – and the reason I had decided to get involved.

Around eighty of these ran at the first camp. As part of the workshop team, this became my primary focus. There were usually seven workshop tents available at any one time, including an impromptu space to be used by people who turned up at the Camp and then asked to do one. We used these spaces for scheduled workshops half the time and kept the rest of the time open for unscheduled ones.

From worker adult education to the civil rights movement, popular education has historically been a crucial element of many social movements. Methods were developed to challenge oppression by syndicalists in the early twentieth Century, and in the 1960s, Paulo Freire from Brazil developed the concept of 'praxis'. By this, he meant the integration of reflection and action, practice and theory, thinking and doing.

Some of that thinking seems to have influenced the camp ethos – all manner of education was on offer. There were four possible workshop slots in a day. So with seven running simultaneously, a maximum of 28 workshops per day was possible. The workshop program ran for three days – so 84 slots were selected by the workshop group; the campers were excellent audiences (plus locals in subsequent camps – this was a year we educated each other).

To me, the most informative of workshops were those dealing with mitigating climate change. I ran one on eco-architecture and attended others on peak oil and green futures. The ethos would be Paul Hawken's: 'Do what needs to be done and check to see if it was impossible only after you are done'.

By concentrating on just a single marker, such as zero-carbon or global warming, other environmental indicators were being ignored – air pollution, for example, from nuclear power or incinerators. As Zac Goldsmith, former editor of the *Ecologist Journal* points out: '…the environment became about carbon, not the environment you can feel and touch and see'. *Pollution, biodiversity, and waste management* would all now play second fiddle to carbon dioxide. 'However, climate change is a huge issue and maybe its impact on the planet is even greater than many issues that we find ourselves in, which in turn is relegating climate change to the global agenda of things to fix!'

Thirty-four people came to my first workshop. It was to discuss how to upgrade existing and new housing to reduce heating bills by 90%. (Eco-architecture). In the UK, the heating of buildings is responsible for around 35% of greenhouse gas emissions. It was only in the previous 2 years that the Government had published guidelines to maximise energy efficiency. Previous 'envelope' type schemes of refurbishment had only marginally reduced their CO^2 or global warming impact – and focused on bringing the old stock up to minimum Building Regulation standard, for example, the replacement of single with double-glazing.

Until recently, Building Regulation standards in this country have lagged behind best EU thermal practices, resulting in a large legacy stock of buildings whose thermal performance has been so poor; the oldest have forced residents to live in what is termed 'fuel poverty'. The result is 17, 000 or more unnecessary deaths every winter (2018-19 figures); it continues to be a national disgrace for the UK, accounting for 10% of carbon emissions.

The EU's 2002 Energy Performance of Buildings Directive (EPBD 2002/91/2002) was a framework directive transposed into national legislation for a new building, (and updated in 2010), implemented by all 27 member countries…All measures are part and parcel of the EU's 20% energy savings target by 2020 from 2007 levels. This implies (worldwide) a carbon emission reduction by a factor of four by 2050 from 1990 levels. The EU missed this target by a whopping 14%.

From 2006 (until its abolition in 2016), an additional standard had been applied to new homes, called the *Code for Sustainable Housing*. It was mandatory for new residential development and was to be progressively applied to a target of carbon neutrality by 2016. The rating system was a six-point scale, from very poor (1) to state-of-the-art (6), similar to that used for fridges but using numbers rather than letters (and working in the reverse order). The abolition of this rating measure was another victim of a bonfire of regulations and quinoas, which started in 2011. Another 'victim' was the Royal Commission on environmental pollution.

At my workshop, I gave a detailed example of how a high-performance residential (level 3) block could be designed. This illustrated some of the trade-offs required to achieve that. It is achievable through detailing. It was a timber-framed FSC (Forestry Council Certified), triple-glazed and had a communal woodchip-burning biomass boiler (at Albion Place in Oxford). These characteristics gave it a lower CO_2 output than gas. In order to design in this way, different design scenarios can be tested in a spreadsheet provided by the code assessor, a Building Research Establishment environmental rating under license.

Whether there is currently a consensus that the buildings sector has to contribute to energy consumption reduction targets, implemented through ambitious, long-term policy, is doubtful. The market illustrates this.

There is a limited choice to the specified. There is little demand for products like triple-glazing (one supplier at the time) and biomass boilers (none then). The reason there is little demand is because we have no tangible policy to build to a higher standard. So these items had to be sourced from Sweden and Slovenia – when they could have been made here. 'Policy priorities need re-setting and there must be a more concerted effort to learn from, and apply best practice policies to deliver this significant mitigation potential from buildings.'

Considerable embodied energy is involved in the demolition of existing terraced housing compared with new-build because it means off-site manufacturing new material – prefabrication. This 'embodied' energy is also another planet-warming issue. Cement manufacture is particularly energy-intensive, with few alternatives (like lime aggregates) available. There is also a massive deficit of skill shortage in refurbishment, which means costs are often substantially higher than new-build. Refurbishment attracts a higher rate of VAT compared to new-build.

One joint session pitched Guardian columnist George Monbiot with Richard Hawkins (from the *Centre for Alternative Technology*). George made the case for a European-wide electrical super grid, using HV direct current technology, in which cables would be used to link all renewable sources in Europe, together with offshore wind farms much further out to sea, Icelandic geothermal, and solar thermal arrays in North Africa, up to 4500Km long. He said this was the time of decision. However, by the following year (Kingsnorth), he was to switch his support to nuclear power, on the basis that '…everything hinges on stopping coal.' Possibly he saw the super grid as politically unrealistic (Arab Spring).

Richard Hawken, by contrast, while not offering any prescriptive solution for carbon reduction; drew attention to the manufacture of solar panels and embodied emissions; the photovoltaic industry is one of the fastest-growing emitters of hexafluoroethane (C_2F_6), nitrogen trifluoride (NF_3) and sulphur hexafluoride (SF_6); three greenhouse gasses that have a global warming potential 10,000 to 24,000 times greater than CO^2 according to the Intergovernmental Panel on Climate Change.

Action Support, on the other hand, offered a practical action-training course in fence climbing. During the last two days, the focus shifted to the action – which I was less comfortable with than the workshops. I had reservations about the target; knowing just how dangerous electricity could be, I warned all and sundry their need to consider personal safety. In the event, the perimeter was secured by force of police numbers, even if wire cutters were planted at points known to the police. Somebody managed to climb a peripheral lighting tower (outside the fence) and that was about it.

Former *NUM* leader Arthur Scargill drew parallels with the miners' strike. 'There are similarities in that they are people who are demonstrating for what they believe in and they are doing so in a way that draws attention to them from the media and from the forces of the state. I find it offensive and obscene that you can have police in the numbers that you had at Climate Camp, particularly riot police, stopping people from entering the field. They are stopping and searching for people going inside and asking for their names and addresses.'

At his workshop, Mr Scargill had given qualified support, stating he couldn't agree with the campaigners' views on coal as a dirty fuel but said that he could see parallels in the cause they were fighting for and the struggle the miners faced in the 1980s.

Not all workshops were as well received in subsequent years, some speakers seemed intent on antagonising the campers. *The Scottish Resources Group*, a coal industry lobby group body (who hired a private investigator to report on the Climate Camp), '...Coal is doing what other fuels are failing to do at this difficult time – helping keep Britain's households lit and warm.' Mr Brewer added: 'It's at times like this that the nation feels the full benefit of a fuel that's easy to transport, handle and store, is abundant in the UK and around the world, flexible in its use and never fails to deliver.' Arthur Scargill would have agreed. Totally the wrong direction, but no censorship anyway.

During the *Red Pepper* workshop, campaigner Kat Ainger had warned us: 'Success is dangerous'. Just at the moment when George Monbiot had this to say: 'you cannot separate capitalism from the issue of control...we have to start from where we are, the circumstances are the ones we have to engage with. Our primary task is to prevent runaway climate change and if it means using the state, then so be it...the question is how to achieve new order against powerful defenders of the status quo'. You are shifting the terms of mainstream debate, you encounter the *sticky embrace* of corporations and the state who will say, 'we want the same things as you'. 'There's a classic PR tactic of defusing movements by co-opting moderates and isolating radicals. And success is heady; it can lead to repetition of tactics that worked once. A movement needs to innovate; literally, to keep moving.' The corollary is it could lead to a 'no platforming' cult. It has led to the *Extinction Rebellion*.

Now, she noted: '...the *Occupy* movements are setting the agenda: rather than being reactive at summits where the powerful determine the terrain, they are occupying in their own neighbourhoods at times of their choosing. And they are staying...'

Backbench MPs were sympathetic to the campers and 227 of them voted against new coal power stations *without carbon capture.* They focused ma matters at the Cabinet-level. It was announced £110Bn worth of new power stations were required over the next decade. At the same time, the go-ahead for a new Kingsnorth power station without being fitted with carbon capture had already been given. The elephant in the room. That majority would never have been achieved without the focus the camp provided.

My personal interest was as a specifier in energy conservation. This could reduce the demand for energy. 'Too often, buildings do not match the original aspirations of designers. This leads to higher-than-expected energy use and emissions. There are many reasons for this, including building energy modelling errors; specification changes before and during construction; rushed or incomplete commissioning; unanticipated occupant behaviour.'

January 2016 saw my involvement with feasibility studies in thermal retrofit. The pilot involved the upgrading of a terrace of Coventry houses to the German 'Passivhaus' standard. At this level of insulation, combined with very low air leakage, heating bills could be cut by a factor of ten; and politically, there was scope for funding from the pot of money accumulated over two decades of council house sales to tenants (which had been locked away). This pilot project went to fruition, and the plan was to roll it out on a larger scale (with state funding), with the benefits of prefabrication of bedroom/dining room pods to the rear of the houses, toilet extensions. The full implementation was never to be rolled out. It suggested ministers had given up on energy efficiency.

Chapter 12

Heathrow (14–21 August 2007)

A recent study claims global tourism (prior to Coronavirus) accounts for 8% of carbon emissions, around three times greater than had previously been thought. Not everyone was happy with the selected target that year: the choice of Heathrow Airport arose from airport expansion, the key issue in 2007. In contrast to the lack of local support at Drax, this campaign would have overwhelming support in the immediate area of London under threat of demolition.

'...It was inevitable that we would be accused of wanting to disrupt holidaymakers.' Two villages were threatened with demolition to make way for the third runway. Heathrow, which had started life as a single runway built in allotments, is one of the busiest airports in the world. The airport location is far from ideal because it is a legacy site, formerly allotment gardens in the conurbation rather than outside it (unlike many others in Europe). Two existing runways are in use at pretty much full capacity between dawn and dusk. It seems that the official aim of all governments has been economic growth and amassing foreign earnings. Reiterating the need for competition with the Paris hub, the expansionist nature of European air travel becomes clear, now dealt a blow by

Coronavirus. When Heathrow's fifth terminal was approved, a planning condition had capped the number of flights using the airport at 480,000 a year. The new runway would then raise that figure to 720,000. Heathrow is also the scene of forced repatriation flights, sending child refugees back to war-torn countries.

Debate on the future of London's airports has been ongoing since the war. British Airways, the largest airline operator at the airport, had previously requested Hillingdon Council not to approve anything which would '…jeopardise future development of a third runway.' Their request came in response to the Hillingdon council's 15-year strategic plan.

The expansion of Gatwick and 'Borris Island', (similar to an earlier proposal at Foulness in the Medway estuary), and another based on the end of the Hoo peninsula near Kingsnorth had all been rejected, partly on safety grounds in relation to a bird strike, which has brought engine failure in estuarial locations.

Some alternative sites were even more remote than the Medway estuary in Kent. One previous SWOT analysis (*Aviation Policy for the Next 30 Years: Airport Development in the UK 2002*) had in fact implicated an area of land nearly one hundred miles away. This implausible location – a plateau between Coventry and Rugby. Under that proposal, Heathrow would have been replaced outright. This had caused a massive amount of planning blight in 2002 in Warwickshire. It had been hugely resented by locals there, who could not understand how such a far-flung location could even have been considered. They felt victimised.

It would have required a high-speed rail link (pre HS2), which was a part of these proposals at that time. It was rejected, after about 2 years of wrangling, as impractical. It was a bizarre choice in the first place.

Globalisation has boosted aviation to a level of mass usage. Whilst accepting it was a consensus decision, criticism of the choice centred on the guilt trip. *The mute magazine* argued that '…instead of showing the interconnectedness of the Social and the Ecological, Climate Camp (had) picked the individual as the point of attack' by focusing on the 'unethical' lifestyle choices of those who fly. I remember a discussion with an activist about his ambitions for what is being dubbed the 'climate movement'. 'To make a lot of people very guilty,' he replied. This emphasis on guilt was the very opposite of what I had hoped for. Actually, just not flying is a reasonable alternative. 'Deal with it.'

Promises were finally broken in 2016, when the Third Heathrow runway had been shortlisted – despite being in breach of our own *Climate Change Act*. It was due to be completed by the end of the decade; now sabotaged by a pandemic.

I think everyone knew we were now in the 'big smoke', the capital of England, and Heathrow was a vitally important campaign for the camp. It was a huge issue to support and we had to deal with it professionally. The media profile at Drax had raised the ante, by securing the first three pages in the *Independent* and having a significant internet profile.

The documents appeared to be so much 'lobby fodder', largely written by BAA; and it seemed to skirt the real impacts. Such a report, reminiscent of the dodgy dossier case for the war in Iraq previously, was greeted with profound scepticism by those locals not employed at the airport, enduring as they had to, planes taking off and landing every minute over a ten-hour day. It also attracted flak from Zac Goldsmith as a local MP. Greenhouse Gas emissions have increased year on year from air travel, for example, from the European Union, by 87% between 1990 and 2006. Aviation had somehow been exempted from the Kyoto Protocol, but *not* the Climate Change Act. The third runway threatened a further CO^2 increase by 7.3million tonnes annually.

Airlines receive over £9 billion in tax breaks each year; tax-free kerosene and VAT-free tickets and planes. UK air travel contributed 13% to UK greenhouse gas emissions in 2005. This was based on departing flights only; however, if the calculation was to be based on return flights by UK citizens in 2007, the figure would be nearer 20% (UK Aviation Minister figures).Astonishingly, the supporting document failed to mention this, while the 2003 White Paper (*Predict and Decide – Aviation, climate change and UK policy*) had proposed that aviation capacity to increase by 200–300% by 2030. This was clearly incompatible with the Government's Climate Change Act. This effectively meant emissions from aviation would have exhausted the UK's entire allowable emissions by 2050. Government support is dependent on a planning application.

When the then Secretary of State, Ruth Kelly, had the opportunity to slap a £100 take-off and landing fee on every aircraft using Heathrow, she chose not to do so. That would instantly have started to signal the extent of the dilemma. At a time when other modes of transport were the subject of Government incentives and regulations (low emission zones) designed to bring about reductions in harmful emissions, there were no similar measures being taken for aviation. Nor were air travellers interviewed at the time concerned about their air travel usage.

Carbon emissions from aviation had grown by about 5% p.a. since 1990, and this was clearly incompatible with the Government target of a 60% reduction in emissions by 2050. (At the same time, many NGOs were calling for a 90% reduction). In 2020, with the two runways, 1300 flights per day have been slashed to a mere 130 during the coronavirus lockdown. These flights are mainly freight.

The debate, like the climate, had heated up that year. The urgency of the situation had turned many individuals and NGOs, like FoE, to look to the state for legislative solutions, such as the *Climate Change Bill*; social change had fallen off the agenda. Climate Camps looked at climate as the symptom of a systemic problem and they wanted to change that system. The camp had attracted many people (including myself) who were more liberal than anarchists. This tension continued to make for lively debate.

In marked contrast to rural Drax, we expected and received a huge number of day visitors – those people were valuable, local residents who would be supportive. Their first point of call would be the information tent where a briefing pack was available. The central kitchen would cater for them – while neighbourhoods had their own kitchens. There was a morning briefing at the same time as the neighbourhood's meeting. Resources were stretched; we asked for a donation to cover meal costs.

For once a condition was to be self-imposed: that while everyone was welcome to come to the camp, *they were not to cross the perimeter fence at Heathrow, where planes are present (runways, taxiways, storage areas and air traffic control) for the entire duration of the camp.* This was to avoid putting the general public and airport staff in danger, and for the safety and security of the camp as a whole. The consultation argument was that an exemption would give the aviation industry time to come up with some miraculous 'green' solution to the air pollution it created; carbon offsetting. The call for demand to be managed, to ensure that environmental impacts were minimised, came from NGOs such as the *Woodland Trust*. Ministers believed that they would need derogation from the EU and tried to put a brave face on it. The researchers from Imperial College London suggested that the strategy to reduce emissions from planes taking off, using a strategy known as 'reduced thrust', has increased fuel efficiency and reduced the levels of the pollutants nitrogen oxide (NO^x) and black carbon.

Air quality is a problem that never goes away in the capital, particularly for nitrogen oxides. And Britain has a mortality rate of 25.7 per 100,000 compared to Sweden's 0.4, it is regularly subject to fines from the EU. Now, as I write, a decade later, we have an about-face. In 2020, though, the outbreak of the coronavirus pandemic has grounded their expansion plans yet again; possibly indefinitely.

Some of Harmondsworth and most of Sipson would have been compulsorily purchased and demolished for the third runway. Although Spanish-owned, Ferrovial had compulsory purchase powers inherited from the Civil Aviation Authority. Some 240 homes in Sipson had been bought over a long time, as they came on the market, through its property bond scheme.

One of the oldest grade II listed churches in the country was scheduled for demolition in the village of

Harmondsworth. The church, and associated graveyard, were to be smack bang at the end of the proposed third runway, which was to finish in the middle of that village! Since then, in its revised incarnation, the runway has been moved closer to the existing terminus. The Church and medieval hammer barn will now be saved (and no graves need to be interred).

The Climate Camp resolved the following *camp objectives for Heathrow:*

- Confront corporate profiteers, like BAA (Spanish parent company Ferrovial) and BA, who were aggressively lobbying for airport expansion and manufacturing our desire to fly.
- Compel government to cancel plans for the third runway, stop airport expansion and reduce capacity in line with climate science limits.
- Raise awareness that flying is the most environmentally destructive lifestyle choice that an individual can make; persuade people to take responsibility for their actions and fly much less.
- Create a space where less was more and find the solutions to our problems in our own communities rather than feeling the need to escape to other parts of the world.

There was understandably, also immense local opposition to further expansion at Heathrow, (except among those employed there). With aircraft already taking off and landing every 60 seconds for ten hours every day, noise disruption was significant, together with the nauseous stench of burnt kerosene. Air quality limits were also borderline on nitrogen oxides.

The London neighbourhood had already delivered 3500 letters to many of the directly affected homes. The police had intimidated those local residents who distributed posters. A 'speed-dating' service hooked up local residents with affinity groups to develop plans to resist evictions. The *BAA p*roperty bond scheme had, at that time, bought up some 240 homes in Sipson as and when they came to the market.

Robbie Gillett, a *Plane Stupid* activist, put it this way: 'The government thought the third runway was a done deal, then suddenly they had 2,000 people on the land saying 'this isn't going to happen'. Greenpeace pitched in with its Airplot group, a legal Deed of Trust containing the names of over 90,000 'airplotters', who became joint beneficial owners of this plot of land. That included LibDem leader Nick Clegg. This has now been abandoned, it had to be renewed annually.

By May 2010, both Prime Minister David Cameron and his then-deputy Nick Clegg had pledged that the third runway at Heathrow would not go ahead; a pledge was included in the coalition agreement. This was a pledge that was never likely to be honoured.

Not only were 15,000 homes and six schools to be blighted by noise, but several hundred buildings were also scheduled for compulsory purchase and demolition. Under the 2016 proposal, the runway was moved marginally nearer to the existing one, to Miss Harmondsworth church and the hammer barn, both of which were grade 1 listed. 'Jim Fitzpatrick, then a transport minister, met the head of BAA a week before Climate Camp protesters held peaceful demonstrations at Heathrow Airport.' By the end of 2007,

106 MPs had signed a motion asking the government not to proceed with the plans for a third runway at Heathrow and to hold a Commons vote on the subject. Now (2020) it is all set to go ahead, but postponed for at least a decade owing to coronavirus.

John McDonnell MP was fulsome in his praise. He said: 'I joined Climate Camp when it came to my area to protest against those who are not content to know, but who are ready to act – and ready to challenge the powerful Heathrow third runway…I learned more about Climate Camp activities than from all the debates in parliament. The Climate Camp…transformed our campaign from a local issue to an internationally renowned campaign, making a pivotal contribution in defeating the third runway.'

The two main opposition groups at that time were *HACAN CLEAR SKIES* (Heathrow Association for the Control of Aircraft Noise) and *NoTRAG*. HACAN was particularly active in terms of lobbying MPs (of whom John McDonnell was a key supporter). The level of frustration felt locally was palpable, as housing was under threat.

Then there was *NoTRAG* (No Third Runway Action Group), a residents group made up of those whose homes and schools would be degraded or destroyed – they lacked access to 'decision makers'. The threat of losing their homes had galvanised these residents, and they wasted no time in mobilising publicity. Heathrow Airport operator, the Spanish-owned multinational Ferrovial, had compulsory purchase powers delegated from the nationalised British Airports Authority.

NoTRAG would achieve international coverage for the first time. With the restrictions placed by the campers on the press, they were clamouring to speak to locals. John Vidal might complain, but both *NOTRAG and HACAN* benefitted from that attention. Meanwhile, the London neighbourhood of our camp attended *NoTRAG*'s AGM so they would know what had been achieved media-wise at Drax (where we had achieved the first three pages in the *Independent* newspaper). Foreign news crews reported parallel news of anti-expansion groups in their own countries, all interested in Sipson's future.

Eight local councils formed their own lobby (the ad hoc '3M' group), also three police forces were involved, so there was a lot to do. There were members of the London neighbourhood to do it, plus others from London 'Rising Tide' group. Jenny Jones, at that time the Green party member of the Metropolitan police authority – had agreed to a suggestion that the Met were to use Operation (*Harmony-2)*, a crowd control plan previously used by the police. And indeed, it was relatively harmonious that year.

HACAN's John Stewart and Sarah Clayton went on to build an international coalition called *AirportWatch*, made up of airport activists with a total membership of 6 million people, working on issues ranging from noise, global justice, to bird protection.

HACAN had been leading critics at the Terminal-5 inquiry and had singled out the consultation as a sham. John Stewart was very charismatic.

A local pub in Sipson was extremely supportive and served many a free pint to their unexpected supporters. This probably did not extend to London Evening Standard journalists, who throughout the camp continued to fabricate 'knocking copy' attacking all those taking part. This finally attracted some attention when one of their journalists was carpeted by the Press Complaints Commission.

The media group was in to control freakery. One frustrated journalist wrote: 'The campers have a schizophrenic relationship with the media. Many of (them) said they didn't want to talk to the press and expressed a cynical disdain for the media – yet the camp, with its staged spectacles and huge banners, is a made-for-the-media protest. When a bunch of photographers gathered around a child and his hippy mother, some campers sneered 'get a real job'. 'The London Evening Standard had published a front-page article, (13 August 2008), which alleged a conspiracy to bring Heathrow Airport to a standstill, titled 'Militants will hit Heathrow'. This, they wrote, would be by means of hoax packages and breaching of the fence. The ASA (Advertising Standards Authority) ruled this to be a clause, one breach of requirements for accuracy. The paper alleged: 'the information came and overheard a conversation. He had failed, it was said, to indicate its insubstantial and alarmist basis. The conversation was denied by the claimant, as was the reported search for weak points in the security fence.

George Monbiot was enthusiastic: 'So what else do the critics of direct action expect us to do? How else do they suggest we drag this issue out of the shadows and thrust it to the front of the public mind?' George called the camp 'better organised, more democratic and more disciplined than any (protest) I have seen...running water, sanitation, hot food twice a day, banks of computers and walkie-talkies, stage lighting, sound systems, even a cinema, were set up in a few hours on unfamiliar ground, in the teeth of police blockades...I left the camp convinced that a new political movement has been born.' However, within a year, he was to change his mind, embracing nuclear power, which would upset the veteran campers. (See Chapter 11)

He is now president of the *Campaign against Climate Change*. Of course, the *Guardian* was also happy to quote camp poet Danny Chivers '...the media interest in Climate Camp generated moved the subject of climate change right up the agenda in people's minds, and got people to really discuss the issues.'

The group taken most seriously by the police was *Plane Stupid*...the British Airport Authority had sought the most unprecedented powers, a High Court injunction to prevent activists even arriving at the camp by public transport; and for my part, the police were doing the same with cars used at the previous camp. They had already stopped myself and Kristoff, the clown, in nearby Hounslow, because his number plate was identified from Drax by their Number-plate Recognition System (ANPR).

Metropolitan police had installed this surveillance camera system (ANPR) back in July 1997. This could automatically read, recognise, and track vehicles by their license number plates. The police wanted the driver's name but would not give the reason.

In December the previous year, *Plane Stupid* had briefly closed down the Stansted Airport. This was the action that led to their successful prohibition from attending Heathrow camp. They had brought concrete blocks and 3m. High builders fenced with them and erected a 'stockade' on the runway. They then chained themselves to it. One of the activists taking part, Lily Kember, aged 21, said they had forced their way in using bolt-cutters while the runway was closed for overnight maintenance work. She said: 'There (are) 54 of us currently occupying a space in the taxi, way about 50 metres from the runway'. Holidaymakers were not impressed, as many flights had to be cancelled.

BAA also wanted the right to bar *anyone* travelling from adjacent railway stations. Their lawyers cited the protection of the *Harassment Act 1997*, which was—as campaigners and media were quick to point out—intended to be used for police stalking. They requested the injunction through their lobby group, *Flying Matters*. It was thrown out by the courts. They had, in hindsight, given the camp the legitimacy it needed. The judiciary did not accede to such a blanket request. All that was achieved was a bar on *Plane Stupid's* two most prominent members – Joss Garman and Leo Murray, together with John Stewart, of *HACAN* (who ignored it anyway and gave a workshop). The camp went ahead! *Plain Stupid*, after being banned from campaigning at Heathrow Airport…went en route to the Airbus Super-jumbo factory. Six campaigners boarded a barge carrying a plane wing from the company plant in Broughton, Flintshire.

A big cardboard installation of an aeroplane featured at the main entrance. Above the open door of the plane that led into the camp, a slogan read: 'Exit the system'. Entering the camp, therefore, enables a visitor to gain perspective on the 'system'. From here, 'the system' could be observed, evaluated and criticised from a fresh perspective.

The *Only Planet* handbook given to visitors stated clearly that any change in the climate does not affect us all equally and made a statistical argument that air travel was a class issue.

The council obviously had health and safety concerns; though there was never any public liability insurance (as before) which was a real risk. The issues of water (paid for), electricity (we make our own), toilets, first aid and fire procedures were all agreed upon in advance. Fresh-piped water came from fire hydrants, electricity from solar panels. We paid for our water that year. Briefing packs were already prepared for chief executives of councils etc. and reps from police forces. We issued them in advance. So the police would see us for the first time in a non-confrontational, organised, professional setting.

The 'site swoop' involved around 150 people. It was timed (as usual) a day before it was expected. The overnight move occupied a field only 850 metres from the Heathrow perimeter itself and erected massive scaffolding tripods.

The Climate Camp media team was cock-a-bull:

'We want to highlight that no Climate Camp has resulted in a conviction for any offence of violence. Every year since the inception of the Climate Camp, the police have warned about lone mavericks with dangerous intents. They have never materialised. Climate change is such an emergency that everyone from Al Gore to NASA's James Hansen, to a jury of ordinary people at Maidstone Crown Court last month is coming out in support of direct action and civil disobedience to prevent it.' (This was referring to a Greenpeace banner drop at Kingsnorth power station).

It had been announced around that time that the Secretary of State, Ruth Kelly, had it in her power to slap a £100 take-off and landing fee on every aircraft using Heathrow from that Monday morning. This would have instantly started to impact positively on climate change, and signal the extent of the problem. Predictably, she chose not to do so, sending a clear message to the local populace that, at heart, the government had no greater interest other than backing the Heathrow Hub.

As previously mentioned, the *BAA p*roperty bond scheme had, at that time, bought up some 240 homes in Sipson as and when they came to the market. With the remaining homes under threat, locals were looking for help from wherever it came. We gave them open access to the workshops, the kids' tent and the cinema tent. Some had accepted personal mentoring under the speed dating style 'Adopt-a-Resident' scheme. Names of residents and activists were drawn from a hat, and each activist pledged to their adopted resident that they would come and support them if the need arose. This image of trust and youth seemed to be a heady mix, helping the residents come to terms with the threat they were experiencing.

A rural site, in a playing field off Sipson Lane, was chosen and a short distance from the village of the same name, which was due to be flattened in order to make way for the third runway. '...the land being squatted by the Climate Camp was part of Harlington Sports Ground. This may have been an astute choice: the sports fields were owned by *Imperial College* and were then under threat of Compulsory Purchase to facilitate Heathrow's expansion. The lane had entrances at either end but the site of that luckily had just the one. It was conveniently located between the airport site and the M4, next door to an unexpected Buddhist temple and other playing fields. But the rear perimeter was unfenced. With a huge (and welcoming) banner strung across two tall tripods of scaffolding poles – it was difficult to miss.

Such a site 'swoop' would never be so easy again; it was a media win.

First up was an entrance tent. This is where newcomers were briefed in small groups regarding the principles and practices of the site and to explain the camp objectives. By night, the site was illuminated by bright spotlights. The visitors thought these had been provided by the campers, though it was in fact the Metropolitan police. It stopped us tripping over the guy ropes, anyway. We did, however, provide our own toilets and marquees.

'Organiser John Jordan confirmed he had sent an email to protesters, urging them to pack formal clothes and air stewardess uniforms. He said protesters might choose to target businesses around Heathrow and will use smart clothing to blend in with ordinary workers'. Not sure that happened. Quite how many were undercover police mingling we will probably never know. There were 1800 'official' police on call and 58 arrests were made during the event.

The power team had a lot of equipment to wire up that year: 14kW of solar panels (in 3 locations) on a ring main, and pedal-powered generators and batteries for the media tent. More power than was needed, anyway.

'Be the Media' fretted about their internet connection. *Psand.net* normally rented a satellite uplink using its own satellite dish; but proximity to Heathrow was a potential safety problem with air traffic control. This was because so many aircraft were in the line of transmission from the geostationary satellite somewhere over the equator. There was talk of having to use mobile broadband. In the event, there were no problems.

As it was at Drax, but on a larger scale, hundreds of tents and numerous marquees were clustered by themes and regions across the available space. These were separated by fire lanes with their flanking barrels of water. Luckily, there were no fires. But if there had been, I believe they could have been contained! Washing areas, compost toilets, a central kitchen/canteen were erected, grouped in previously agreed regions. Moreover, because of detailed advanced planning, it was not apparent how the camp functioned.

One huge marquee that year was devoted to workshops and social events, with split curtains dividing the space up. This, unfortunately, led to a noise breakthrough. Separate marquees had been used to eliminate cross-talk between six workshops the previous year.

'The length of the meetings (at Heathrow) is becoming increasingly annoying. They started off at about an hour, now they are running up to two hours each. It seems most of the day is taken up by non-stop meetings. This has reached farcical proportions because last night there was a meeting that went on from 6 pm until 11 pm (5 hours) with an interruption for a speech by George Monbiot.' Neighbourhoods (or *barrios*) were responsible for staffing the gate for 24 hours periods (with six people per rota). The Gate working group had been briefed a month before the Camp and ran a training session each lunchtime for their replacements. Each determined what issues it wished to bring to the attention of the camp each day and sent representatives to a morning council. Subject matter ranged from where the crèche toilets should be positioned to what statements, if any, should be made to the press during the daily briefing at 11 am. It is disappointing to report that a number of wheelie bins on site had street numbers on them, suggesting they had been 'borrowed' from local addresses.

Mark Kennedy was there '…involved peripherally with the "land group" calculating transport logistics. Nice to have a pro policeman doing that! He drove a box truck full of action equipment and stuff for securing the site.'

There was much concern among camp veterans about a "false flag" incident in which a group left to join what they understood to be a protest at Hatton Cross, organised by locals, on 15 August. They soon discovered that the locals hadn't organised it; they were rapidly rounded up by police and kettled. They claim they were then marched off by police to be corralled on the Bath Road, which was then reported by the media as the first evidence of the demonstrators disrupting passengers' lives.

This incident heightened the theatrical relation between media and police. The Camp response was to monitor police activities through *CopWatch*. Blanket restrictions by the camp media team were unworkable. This was proven when the *Daily Telegraph* reported overnight the result of a vote before the press release from the campers. This was the choice adopted for the day of action.

Back on-site, there were more day visitors than in previous years. Some of the campers seemed to believe that there were two undercover police officers for each camper – but that seemed unduly paranoid to me. Veteran environmental expert Dr Mayer Hillman had to compete with the noise of a police helicopter for two hours in a packed marquee. When members of the audience intervened on his behalf, they were bluntly told 'no', police 'have a job to do'.

The *BAA* headquarters (The *Compass Centre*) was targeted for a blockade on the day of action (noon Sunday to noon Monday). The route there was a long circular that took in both Sipson and Harmondsworth. Just after midday, the kids and parents March along with the Rinky Dink bicycle Sound system set off on the march to Sipson Village. A 'funeral' procession and a 'monstrous plane' figure (assembled by kids and parents in the days before) completed the tableaux. Further locals joined at the camp gates. The march to the village was a very stop-start affair, and heavily cordoned. Police vans in front of the kids march and behind effectively 'kettled' them; meant nobody could leave. This was presumably to deter breakaway groups.

Finally, the 'block' of kids reached the local garden centre. However, because of the force of numbers, a much longer delay ensued. This was resolved by local MP John McDonald, who pleaded with the police for the march to be allowed to continue at Harmondsworth.

Face boxes were used as part of this action. These face shields featured large-scale pictures of real people whose lives had been adversely affected by climate change. These images were pasted onto cardboard boxes, and handles were attached to the sides. Inside the cardboard boxes was not only stuffing to protect campers from police batons but pop-up tents that were to be used to camp at *BAA*. The *Occupy* movement has also adopted this tactic.

The *Clown Army* lightened the atmosphere with playful jesting. 'Going on e-mission: carbon catching, using fishing rods baited with broccoli, lassos, and butterfly net'. To quote their former website: 'Though they didn't catch much carbon, they did catch the forces of darkness out on several occasions: taking a bus to avoid capture by panting policemen, escaping a police kettle (encirclement) by ducking through a hedge, breaking out of the circle of riot police, being a singing clown toilet for trapped demonstrators'.

Speakers were lined up on the village green, Harmondsworth, where speeches were made starting with John McDonald. He thanked the Camp for Climate Action for choosing this project, as well as berating the destruction of two villages, before declaring 'No third runway, we will win'. Next up was Christine Shilling from *NoTRAG* – No Third Runway Action group.

After the speeches, some families left and headed back, while the majority of the campers decided to go to Compass House, BAA HQ. Residents and their children did not, by contrast, attract any further police attention and they returned to their homes. For the activists, a long, heavily kettled circular route agreed, was south to the A4 near the western end of the runway and then heading eastwards down the A4, straight back to BAA HQ, which was about 2 miles. This was to be the setting for a 24-hour sit-in in their car park. No comfort stops were permitted. One woman had to urinate on the road surface. Both edges of the road were flanked by an unbroken cordon of police, and the eastbound lane of the dual carriageway was closed to traffic to allow us to continue.

'About 250 climate change campaigners spent last night camping in tents in the BAA's car park. It was surrounded by riot police. A scuffle broke out in which there were a number of injuries, and it looked like the BAA blockade would be driven back to camp (half a mile away) by late evening.'

141

Not everyone was convinced this was worthwhile...one blogger wrote: 'The ritual of marching on the headquarters of *BAA* seems to be no more than a case of presenting oneself for temporary encirclement by a cordon of police officers, and submitting oneself to the gaze of the media. It's less a case of misfortune, and a more direct consequence of the mental and physical asceticism of the camp that the banner which dominated later news photos claimed the movement's desire was to "Make Planes History".'

A splinter (affinity) group had gone in a different direction, to the outside of the airport, occupying the access road leading to the warehouse that handles perishables flown in from across the world. The police thought this was the main action and diverted their resources and top officers away from the several hundred people at the BAA office, to a mere fifteen strong affinity groups that had blocked the perishables access road to the freight terminal.

They had hit a target that Heathrow was the more concerned about. The cargo centre was rumoured to be closed for the weekend. Despite the economic cost of closure, charges were dropped against those who had been locked down there.

Meanwhile, those at the BAA HQ used the respite to settle in for the night, with their pop-up tent backpacks. The HQ was encircled by the TSG, BAA had, as a precaution, moved its operations inside the perimeter fence of the airport. At the same time, diverse affinity groups were busy with more office occupations in London, including one at the office of *Bridgepoint Capital*, new owners of Leeds Bradford airport, a regional airport also seeking to expand. 17 August also saw XL Airways at Gatwick occupied, (the UK's second-biggest airport).

Numerous travel agencies were blockaded with heavy chains across their doors, and ten people barricaded the UK's Department for Transport, which was encouraging airport expansion. One of these ten was a Latvian tourist—not connected with the Climate Camp—who was so inspired by the action that he locked onto another door of his own accord. Another of these activists was an undercover clown—'officer A'—'Lynn Watson' (real name unknown).

The next day (18 August) saw more of the same affinity group actions. Forty people shut down *Carmel Agrexco*—an Israeli-owned company specialising in airfreighting food from illegally occupied Palestine—for three hours. At the same time, 'Bicycology' worked on outreach in the local area while other activists supported a strike over the working conditions of Heathrow's baggage handlers. Children at the camp got together and did their own blockade at the World Freight Centre to the south of the airport.

In May 2010, the airport's operator *BAA* dropped plans for new runways at Heathrow and Stansted airports, bringing to a close one of the most controversial parts of the previous Labour government transport policy. Aviation Minister Theresa Villiers also issued a written statement to confirm that the Government has dropped a third runway and 'mixed mode' at Heathrow Airport. Since then, it has been re-approved and then postponed. There was no government support for expansion in 2019, and very little air travel in 2020, anyway. A further planning application seems very unlikely before 2030.

One of the more endearing spin-off projects from that year was set on one of those pieces of derelict land that *BAA* intended compulsorily purchase to make way for the expansion – the *Grow Heathrow* project. Before activists arrived, the derelict greenhouses were used as a dumpsite. On 1 March 2010, six community members occupied what had become a scrap yard. 'Growing food is seen as more positive than blocking aircraft,' they said. Since the runway was cancelled, the site's owners have registered an interest in seizing back the land. In 2011, the gardeners were served with legal proceedings for eviction, but they were still there as of 2019.

The project had, in its time, provided local residents with a space to start building more sustainable communities after the third runway was dropped in March 2010. *Grow Heathrow* gardeners and local residents have had to clear some 30 tonnes of refuse with the help of the local council and carefully restore the glass in the greenhouses, turning the land back into a market garden and a meeting space for local people.

The market garden is now established, but already under threat of eviction. It will no longer be spared if the third runway is approved; the original owner has an eviction order served. As one local resident saw it: '*Grow Heathrow* is a great example of how an interested party of dedicated individuals (that) has really made a difference in a devastated community…It is groups of similar young people that will be the driving force behind the new government's 'Big Society' idea – as it is only they that will have the drive to try such difficult projects out. Who else would have spent an inordinate amount of time cleaning such a toxic tip as the site in Sipson – when the locals had had so much trouble with it and council had washed their hands of it? They should be given a medal and the site compulsory-purchased on their behalf by the local borough. Why would that happen? In reality, the site has now been partially repossessed. The remainder is the subject of a court order.

'I sincerely wish the *Grow Heathrow* project well in their bid against eviction – as a shining light of what can be done with lots of vision and very little money.' However, in April 2011, *Grow Heathrow* became one of three squats across London to be raided by riot cops, prior to the Royal Wedding. Squatters were dragged out of their beds and searched. An hour and a half later, police left with nothing. It seems possible this was in breach of the law. John McDonald told the press 'I am anxious about it, this is a group of young people who have made a great contribution to revitalise Sipson. They are extraordinarily nice young people who have turned a derelict site into a real community garden.' Meanwhile, back at Kingsnorth, a protester had scaled two 3m razor-wired and electrified fences to single-handedly shut down a 500MW turbine in a massive security breach at the power station. The intruder left a placard at the scene declaring 'No New Coal'. The turbine was shut down for four hours, cutting UK carbon output by 2 percent. Other actions included:

- Five protesters in a banner drop at Sizewell A and B nuclear power stations. Their banner declared, 'Nuclear power is not the answer to climate chaos'.

- Twelve protesters super-gluing themselves to the entrance of the BP HQ. They were highlighting BP's supply role to the aviation industry.
- Eighteen protesters occupying the office of the owners of Leeds airport, *Bridgepoint Capital*, on Warwick Street in London.
- Fifteen protesters occupied the Oxford headquarters of Climate Care, the company which ran British airways carbon-offsetting scheme. Dressed as red herrings, the protesters entered offices and delivered a report called 'The Carbon Neutral Myth', produced by Carbon Trade Watch. They had a two-hour roundtable discussion with the managing director and other senior staff.

The campaign against aviation expansion continued internationally. John Stewart of *AirportWatch* launched his *Aviation Justice Express* tour in the USA in October 2011. There are reported to be some 3,400 airports under construction, expansion, and development projects planned in that country. He took the same template and his experience over there. Americans continue to fly short distances in the USA – because there is no integrated sustainable land-bound public transport (other than greyhound buses and the odd train route). American campaigners were eager to know how Heathrow campaigners had challenged the economic case for a third runway at Heathrow, helping persuade a Conservative-led government to drop it (in 2011).

I believe the UK government was uneasy about climate protest as it drew attention to policy deficiencies. The same issue is apparent in air pollution and diesel scrappage proposals, as I write. On the other hand, the nuclear lobby has benefited from the protest against coal emissions. This issue would never go away for the campers either—as both George Monbiot, James Lovelock and Mark Lynas, media stars, signed up for that radioactive option in the years to follow—in their belief that low CO_2 technology was the 'only game in town'.

BAA may believe carbon offsetting is the way forward. That strategy at London Heathrow Airport is reaching the limit of technology, so further decreases in emissions will have to be achieved by improvements to engine technologies. In 2020, though, the outbreak of the coronavirus pandemic has once again grounded their expansion plans. Many businesses are now used to a meeting by video-conferencing and the aerospace industry may find the market has dropped away from them.

Chapter 13

Kingsnorth Power Station
(Kent, August 2008)

The Government's lack of energy strategy met its denouement in 2008 with the threat of losing 'base load' capacity – or 'lights going out'. The reason for this was threefold; a failure to build new capacity, along with decommissioning of ageing nuclear power plants from 2016, and the proposed closure of coal-powered stations to meet the *Greenhouse Gas Emissions Directive*. Central to this lack of direction was the privatisation of the electricity system in 1998, previously known as the Central Electricity Generating Board, which resulted in an oligarchy called the 'big six'.

The existing plant, located on the River Medway, is the second-highest emitter of CO^2 in England after Drax, (which is more recent technology). Instead, its replacement was to be more efficient *and* 'carbon capture ready'. This is like building a drive and saying it is 'Ferrari-ready'.

Kingsnorth was the most difficult encampment to date. Lodge Hill, as an SSSI, featured a problem 'backdoor', and an impossibly long perimeter (over 1.5km) to secure. Our camp occupied a mere one-third of the available sheep pasture, about 3 miles distant from the power station. It was fringed by dense woodland. This back access was staked out by riot police for the first three days. Worse still, it was MOD owned land. It is the only site of Special Scientific Interest in the country set up to protect nightingales. Watchtowers had to be built and scaffold pole tripods at the back door to try and see what was going on, as being on the brow of a hill, it was not possible to get a line of sight to the north side any other way. The police entered the site under the pretext that some of the vehicles on site were stolen; though this seemed spurious as their owners were asleep in them.

The event that most concerned the police took place in June; when 28 activists in Drax had attached a climbing rope to a coal train's wheels to lock it to adjacent bridge girders. The ropes used could risk damage to the train or bridge if any attempt was made to pull off. Transport police arrested them. As retribution, access to food was cut off by police as they attempted to starve out some of the environmental protesters when they attempted to join the protest in Kent.

Exclusion orders were placed on these particular protesters to bar them from any power station. Paul Morrozzo was the only one arrested and imprisoned when he arrived at Kingsnorth, but then he had already tipped off the police to announce he was coming! Four others managed to sneak in without being spotted, again breaking bail. I believe this may have prompted police to attempt to starve the protest to a halt after the second day and to designate the camp as 'illegal.'

The last thing, therefore, that climate campers needed to hear were journalists they had respected, such as George Monbiot and Mark Lynas, endorsing state-controlled nuclear power solutions (or what was euphemistically described as 'fourth generation' reactors, unproven designs still at the prototype stage). It was this continual focus on life-cycle low-carbon without regard to consequences that caused this. For energy companies such as E.On, it was about dealing with base load demand in time for the ongoing decline in nuclear output. The proposal to build seven newly built coal-fired stations—without any carbon capture and storage—was, for them, risk-free proven technology. The replacement Kingsnorth power station was to be the first of these. Yet, despite the latest high-pressure design technology, it was not expected to be more than 50% efficient – perhaps around 20% better than what it was replacing! According to the *World Development Movement,* 'The new power station planned for Kingsnorth would output more CO^2 each year than the whole of Tanzania.'

Many campers were interviewed on their views as part of a university-led survey. They were deeply unhappy with carbon capture, arguing that it would not work and decrying the way it legitimised the building of more coal-fired power stations and 'business as usual', rather than a managing demand for energy.

John Hutton, then Business Secretary, had no time for the naysayers. He was obviously more concerned about 'lights going out' when he said '...stopping the building of new coal-fired power stations would make no difference to the UK's total carbon emissions but it would, I believe, damage our energy security.' Nuclear power is costly and time consuming to the commission. E.On attempted to be conciliatory: 'If the climate campers want their lives powered solely by renewable energy then E.On can oblige – we are already one of the UK's leading green generators and we have a development portfolio that could provide power for 1million homes and displace 2 million tonnes of CO^2 a year'.

'But it will require much more than just renewable power to secure our energy future and keep prices affordable. By now the UK should have replaced about a third of its existing electricity generating capacity. That is an unprecedented and enormously expensive challenge'. The cost is being passed on to consumers in their energy bills. The EU target of 20% reduction was missed by 14%.

Many climate campers might have hoped that a combination of wind and wave power with increased energy efficiency would be enough to bridge the gap. E.On did not: 'But that is simply unrealistic. We also need a new generation of nuclear reactors, more gas storage facilities and gas stations, and a limited number of new coal-fired stations built *ready to be fitted with CCS equipment*, which *could* cut carbon emissions by 90%'. Asked to explain, *Edelman's*, their PR Company, invented the concept of a 'trilemma'. This they defined as a dilemma in three parts. '…which would only enable E.On to increase their renewable output to 24% by 2030. The key points were: reliability, affordability and climate change. At Drax, wood pellets have replaced a large proportion of the coal. Because it had no track record, Carbon Capture and Storage (CCS) was not an option the DTI could make mandatory. A proposed pilot scheme at Longannet power station in Scotland did not proceed for economic reasons, but there are overseas examples.

CCS would reduce generating efficiency and does not remove all CO^2. It involves condensing CO^2 and burying it in either salt aquifers or partially used oil and gas wells. They want to talk about CCS but the real issue is burning coal, which is what Kingsnorth will be doing in spade-fulls (well ship-fulls). Even in the unlikely event that they do successfully build a CCS section to the plant, Kingsnorth will still emit 6 million tonnes of CO^2 a year. That's a lot more than the third runway at Heathrow would produce.

There are 3 main methods of Carbon Capture and storage:

1. *Pre-combustion capture* involves gasifying the fuel to separate it into hydrogen and carbon dioxide. The hydrogen is lighter, so the two gases are easily separated and the carbon dioxide stream is relatively pure. The hydrogen is then burnt to power a generator and produce electricity. This is the most resource-efficient of the options.

2. *Post-combustion* capture chemically 'scrubs' the carbon dioxide from the mixture of gases produced during the combustion process. This has the advantage that it can be retrofitted to an existing plant. This was the method proposed for the Longannet power station trial in Scotland.

3. *Oxyfuel combustion* involves burning the fuel in oxygen rather than air, meaning that the exhaust gas consists primarily of water vapour and carbon dioxide. When the water vapour is condensed out, the remaining carbon dioxide gas can be captured.

The outcome in 2012 was the decision to extend the life of six nuclear power stations. The direction of energy policy still appears confused. The Department of Energy and Climate Change (DEFRA) is now pinning its hopes on a mix of nuclear, offshore wind and gas-fired power stations, with carbon price floors and 'contracts for difference' as mechanisms, which will see consumers end up footing the bill for a low-carbon generation. The Hinkley Point reactor project is a case in point; electricity generated will be sold at £96 per MWhr.

E.On stated: 'Renewables are low carbon energy sources, emitting the least amount of CO^2. However, they can be intermittent, which is true of wind and sun, for example. We're spending £7 billion globally on lower-carbon technologies, but investing in other forms of energy too to make sure we have energy when we need it. By 2050, the UK government wants Britain to have reduced carbon emissions by 80%, with 15% of total energy from renewable sources by 2020.'

227 MPs signed the early day motion, calling for new coal power stations to be scrapped. It would not be until July 2011 that Government policy required all new coal-fired generating stations to capture and store their carbon emissions 'from a substantial proportion of their capacity'. Sure enough, none has been built. CO^2 accounts for only about 15 percent of the volume of the flue gas from a pulverised coal-fired power plant. The intended retrofitting of Longannet, a power station in Scotland, has been abandoned.

The resources of 24 police forces were thrown behind the policing of the Kingsnorth camp – at, it has been revealed, an eye-watering cost of £5.3m, which involved around 1400 police from as far away as South Wales working 24 hours in a five-shift system. The majority of this (£3.7m) was paid from the national Home Office budget, and the remainder by Kent police, who had been liaising with E.On in advance.

'At Drax, the police were somewhat confused, but by Heathrow, they had become much more strategic and at Kingsnorth, they took that to a new level,' wrote Kevin Smith. **The police chose a confiscation strategy.** As the camp website itself had asked people to bring items to bring to scale and tear down fences, this was hardly unexpected. E.On for their part, in discussion with the DTI (now DECC) about the new power station as well. This was going to be the latest high-pressure technology – but still without carbon capture. They claimed it would be much more efficient than the previous power station.

From Strood railway station, a bus shuttle was run to the site by the campers. This was powered by recycled vegetable oil. The police maintained this to be an illegal taxi service. The camp was rural and clustered into regional neighbourhoods. For their part, the campers had a paltry £12,500 in the bank after all debts from the previous year were settled. The land group fell back on their second-choice site, a huge sheep pasture on Four Elms Hill. This land the farmer leased from the Ministry of Defence. Our main water supply was connected by Southern Water a day or so beforehand, as previously described, from the nearest fire hydrant.

We were joined by a travelling group known as the 'Coal Caravan', a carbon-neutral group of cyclists not caravans, from all over the country who set out through central London and made their way along the Thames valley through Essex, leafleting on the way. Founded by Chris Keene, a Green party activist, this was a peloton (termed 'Bicycology') much like a pilgrimage of old. The 'caravan' was inspired by opposition to opencast coal mining in Southern Scotland and South Wales.

Around 1,400 officers encircled us (in a five shift system), with the constant harassment of campers, journalists and visitors alike. A police helicopter constantly circled overhead, there were systematic searches of people entering or leaving the camp, allegations of a strip search, even claims of 'sexual assault' of women protesters by female police in front of male officers, confiscations of camping equipment, including children's crayons and bike locks (and the bikes they were attached to), the arrest of protesters for a variety of generally vexatious charges, and the bailing condition that they arrestees should not re-enter the Hoo peninsula for the duration of the Climate Camp. As one camper observed: 'We had two police invasions yesterday. Riot cops used pepper spray and batons to batter my friends over the head as they peacefully stood in front of the riot shields, attempting to keep them off our green, pleasant and utterly legal site...I think it means we might be getting somewhere!'

According to Kent Police, the primary goal of 'Operation Oasis' was to pre-emptively seize items that might be used in actions *in preference to arrest the individuals concerned*. MP David Howarth maintained police confiscated items to 'intimidate' protesters at the Climate Camp in Kingsnorth. Freedom of Information request showed items taken included blankets, a walking stick, a clown outfit and soap. This was not, however, made clear to the campers, who were merely handed a little pink chit. This outlined just which of their civil liberties had been suspended and why. This did not go down well.

Kent Police continued to maintain their aim was to 'enable a lawful and peaceful protest'.

According to the official report, the aims of the police operation were:

- The protection of life
- The prevention of crime and disorder
- The facilitation of lawful protest
- The investigation of criminality
- Minimisation of disruption to the local community
- To ensure a swift return to normality

A second (inner) perimeter fence at Kingsnorth had already been erected, and E.On UK was granted an injunction, banning protesters from breaching it and entering the site. Everyone was stopped and searched on the way in, in the 'Tactical Holding Area'. Kent Police erected a large canopy in Deangate Golf Club's car park. Issuing search receipts which were checked again halfway up the lane to the Climate Camp, then again at the entrance to the Climate Camp – which slowed set up quite a lot.

The Camp police liaison group was often being faced with ultimatums; in particular the constant threat of camp invasion. Police claimed that various weapons had been found in the adjacent wood on the western boundary. It was claimed the 'stash' contained an 'adapted' knife which was found in a tree, a replica throwing star, a knife block containing knives and a large chain with a padlock. Whether that was true, it is impossible to know. It was part of an ongoing campaign of slander.

On Monday 4 August, seven members of the affinity group who had stopped a coal train at Drax the year before openly defied bail conditions banning them from the Kent camp. Despite the stop and search policy of the locked-down camp, six of them managed to enter the Camp, despite the ring of blue. The exception was James Thorne, who was caught and jailed in Elmley prison.

Earlier in the year, there had been a model action: 'One of the marked successes in the campaign against Kingsnorth…was the acquittal of six Greenpeace activists who scaled and daubed a message on the chimney during the 2008 Camp for Climate Action at Maidstone Crown court. The case hinged on the justification of 'lawful excuse' – that greater damage would be exacted by the carbon emitted at the successor plant. The valued testament of James Hansen, an eminent NASA climate scientist.' was significant.

That excuse was a 'defence based on necessity'. 'A person shall have a lawful excuse if he damages property in order to protect property belonging to another and at the time of the act he believed (1) that the property was in immediate need of protection and (2) that the means of protection adopted were reasonable having regard to all the circumstances.'

The least provocative (and media-friendly) autonomous action was, however, the symbolism inherent in the targeting of Legoland. '…It all happened earlier this week only in miniature, as Lego campaigners struck at…Legoland, where the cooling tower model was quickly occupied by one-inch-high protesters, all with fixed expressions on their faces. The plastic activists wanted to complete the eerily realistic scene, so Lego police were swiftly in attendance at the foot of the tower.' Legoland staff are now on high alert in case thousands more disgruntled Lego people descend on the site and have called in Lego police from setting around the country to help clamp down on any protest. Ha ha!

The confiscation of bikes caused particular resentment (not mentioned in the Review). D-locks were confiscated because they might be used for 'locking on' at protests. At one point during the week, the police permitted bikes to be locked to the railings of the Golf Club search point. Without any prior warning to the Camp given, the police cut through the D-locks using angle-grinders and seized the bikes. Subsequently, the police offered compensation, saying that there had been a 'failure of communication' and making out it was the Golf Club that had required their removal. Eventually, the bikes (but not the locks!), could be collected from Maidstone police station, on the production of name and address. This was another deliberate attempt to add to the activist database.

They did break into several of the vans, which they were entitled to search in connection with 'criminal activity without evidence'. We had frequent stand-offs with them inside the 'back gate'. One moment it was good cop/bad cop—friendly one minute—and then back to riot gear in another. Then just as suddenly as they had come, they vanished three days and nights later. Inexplicably, journalists seemed to be particularly targeted by the police; some assaults were witnessed; a bad press resulted. There were at least six mainstream journalists on site that year. After several unpleasant confrontations involving the alleged 'stolen' vehicles, it was proposed that two uniformed officers would henceforth have the right to patrol the camp. They were to be accompanied by a couple of volunteers who would shadow them. The police told the media their need patrols were needed to 'protect' visitors from the protesters' as if one was somehow threatened by the other. Another repeated TV theme was the police statement that, 150 *hard-core activists,* were embedded in the camp. They had been saying much the same since Stirling, at which there had been a glimmer of truth. The question could easily have been turned around: how many undercover cops?

A police helicopter hovered above us for hours on end, stopping only to refuel. It was a particular noise nuisance during lecture sessions in the afternoons and when I was trying to get to sleep. In the night, a passing police car played the Clash 'I fought the Law and the Law won' and 'Flight of the Valkyries', on the adjacent road up to nearby Four Elms Hill (though at least there was a sense of humour there). This was at 2.20 am on the morning of Wednesday 6 August when a convoy of police cars sped down the road; then the helicopter arrived and stayed overhead for most of the night. The need for helicopter deployment was also to be questioned in the subsequent police evaluation.

The upshot was a standoff that lasted three days. There were frequent panic call-outs, usually early in the dawn at our back gate, baton-and-shield 'clearances' with at least 30 police, members of the *Tactical Support Group* in full riot gear. Generally, about 50 campers responded. They would rush up to meet them. It was also uncomfortably close for us from our tented area. The tactic used by campers was either a face-off, hands raised in the air, not touching the police; or sitting down refusing to move out of their way when ordered to non-violent resistance. It could become quite heated and there could be a scuffle, once it turned into a rugby scrum. The lack of a clear police Conflict Management model on the ground was apparent.

'Passive resistance' is an age-old protest technique used to slow down removal from a protest. It dates back to CND. Essentially, in '...the sitting position, relaxing muscles so that you go limp. This makes it much more difficult for police to get a handhold, which would involve several officers to remove each person'. Relaxed muscles also hurt less when they suffer rough handling. In my experience, there are few things more intimidating than an advancing line of fully suited, helmeted, baton-wielding riot police. They move forward with the full weight of the state behind them (if not the law) and stomp or beat everything in their path with a chilling methodical certainty. Charging riot police is meant to activate our deepest fight-or-flight instincts. You have to stand your ground, putting your hands in the air and chanting 'This is not a riot'. De-escalation is also a key component (and hopefully result) of this tactic. '...this is not a riot' tactic took hold among members of a Climate Camp confronting police trying to enter the camp.

That camp saw the first electric ring main, including the multi-kilowatt *Generator X* solar truck from Hebden Bridge, augmented by numerous wind turbines, which were used to power the main marquee and the internet. There was no backup that year. The *Be the Media* team were greatly hindered by police confiscation of some of their UHF satellite connectors, though. Police had, by day 3, extended their stop and search powers to 'anyone on the Hoo peninsula'. $60 of the *Criminal Justice and Public Order Act 1994* requires police officers to have 'reasonable suspicion' that an individual is carrying prohibited weapons or articles that could be used to cause criminal damage'.

This had clearly contravened the intended scope of the legislation. The legal team was furious and eventually won their test case in court, in a case that had involved searching of young teenagers. It would take until 14 June 2010 for Kent Police to admit that their stop and searches were 'unlawful' and 'should not have happened'. Three of the campers went on to receive compensation.

A Government statement in the House of Commons from then Police Minister Vernon Coaker backfired when he claimed 70 officers had been injured tackling campers – but it later turned out that this figure was of entirely incidental injuries, including sunstroke and a 'suspected wasp sting', and the minister then had to retract his statement.

The wide-ranging workshop program continued. Once again, I ran my workshop on 'eco-architecture', (see chapter on workshops). I said that there was considerable support for taking community control of energy and that should include pushing for more insulation and energy-efficient heating, without the need for going back to the Stone Age.

Some workshops moved outside, to the back gate, as it was thought officers coming on shift might want to know more about the issues. The camp radio station was used to broadcast what had happened on the previous shift for the benefit of new-coming police.

Paul Chatterton, a Leeds activist and University academic, gave a well-reasoned presentation about the need for a 'just transition'. After underlining the importance of avoiding a climate change 'tipping point' of a four degrees rise, he emphasised that environmentally based politics were ultimately against 'mindless, ceaseless growth' in the form of Neo-liberal capitalism. 'Just transition' would share out the costs of climate change equally, through a 'green new deal', ecological Keynesianism creating a 'green collar economy'. This would amount to the re-nationalisation of energy production and a rejection of the current privatised energy market.

A more controversial topic was *Tradable Energy Quotas*, a scheme devised by other academics in which all citizens were given a quota of energy and large energy users could buy extra energy from those who use less energy. Apparently, DEFRA were currently conducting their own feasibility study into this idea. This workshop attracted considerable hostility, firstly because it was a state-led solution and also offended liberal sensibilities. One camper protested:

'A (*green new deal*) would be compatible with the development of an authoritarian, bio-political state, obsessed with the administration of life. It is quite easy to imagine a dystopian green new deal that continued the valorisation of capital alongside a work-ethic based morality all too conducive to the more sanctimonious elements of environmentalism.' That ill-fated Green New Deal finally was set up in October 2012.

Following this, '...an open letter to the neighbourhoods' was circulated, authored by '...a large group of anti-authoritarian participants in the Climate Camp', and expressing 'deep concern about the direction that the debates have taken over the past days'. It went on to claim that 'In more than one workshop we have heard calls from the podium for *command-and-control* and *market-orientated measures* to address climate change' and 'the responses to these proposals have been far too polite'. Calling for 'A very clear rejection of capitalism, imperialism and feudalism' as well as 'all forms and systems of domination and discrimination' it emphasised 'A *confrontational attitude*, since we do not think that lobbying can have a major impact in such biased and undemocratic organisations'. Was this the earliest example of 'no-platforming?'

The letter did hit on a central issue for the running of the camp: how to both make it 'a welcoming and non-sectarian space' for people new to anarchist ideas, whilst ensuring that career environmentalists didn't get an easy ride. This dilemma was never really resolved, as I will now explain.

While George Monbiot claimed that anarchists were hijacking the movement against climate change, I must admit I was dismayed. Without the anarchists, the event he had previously praised could never have taken place. 'Anarchy is the pursuit of expressive authenticity is a form of protest against disenchantment, which is brought about by the rationalisation of the life world.' Anarchy can work fast too, and not just when riot police arrive on-site at 5.30 am. Perhaps the best example of this took place on the final Sunday evening when a trail of wooden boards that snaked through the camp needed to be stacked. Someone took the initiative to do this, then someone else joined in next to them. Within a couple of minutes, the idea of stacking had gone along the trail, and about a quarter of an hour later it was all done. Quite a strenuous task had been quickly completed, without a single instruction being given.

The day of direct action proper was every bit as traumatic as I had expected. The family-friendly 'orange block' was led by the very visual fancy-dress Chinese dragon, who 'ate coal'. There were up to 1000 parents and children in all, walking to the gates of the power station, where they took a packed lunch. The Camp's Christian Cafe crew held a service giving the power station its last rites. After an hour for lunch, a police helicopter circling above had demanded through a loud haler that they disperse, threatening them with 'horses and dogs' if they didn't. So what had been a peaceful march through various villages on the way turned abruptly and unnecessarily unpleasant on the way back.

I decided to stay behind to help run the camp. A skeleton crew had to remain to man the camp in the absence of the orange block. In a way, they were just a diversion for the more radical *affinity groups* – whether by water, land. Or even air: The blue and IKEA group: water; the green group: hard-core overland, leaving from the back of the camp along the route of a pipeline that was being constructed.

The 123 strong Rebel Raft Regatta took up what I suppose could be described as the scrapyard challenge. They had set out on rafts and canoes. The rafts were made of makeshift pallets and buoyancy barrels sequestered at a boathouse somewhere on the Medway estuary. On Saturday (9 August), four canoeists managed to reach the cooling water intake. The Medway harbour master had invoked a local by-law to ban all boats on the river and most boats were detained.

E.On denied the power station was shut down, but I do not believe this to be true. E.On had instructed 'the water inlet cooling system to be shut down' – no doubt concerned that kayaks might be sucked up by their water intakes. Three of the canoeists were released later on that night and the fourth was charged in the early hours of Sunday morning. He was remanded and bailed, following court on the following Monday.

The silver group was to be airborne, quite the most stupid idea I heard at any camp. I think high-tension cables and, I would like to think, a glimmer of common sense, led to that idea being abandoned. The police helicopter hovered above all week, (reminding me of the G8 at Gleneagles) its first use at a Climate Camp, hovering over the site at great expense, disrupting workshops and sleep alike. It was not clear what purpose this served. The workshop speakers cursed them and it went on, well into the early hours, disrupting all possibility of getting a good night's sleep. The weather turned by day 4 and we had an almighty thunderstorm. Luckily, the chalky ground easily soaked up the rain.

An evaluation of *Operation Oasis* was carried out by South Yorkshire Police. It largely exonerated the Kent strategy but noted that decisions had been made *ad hoc* on the ground without reference to the command chain. Liberal Democrats justice spokesman David Howarth did, however, obtain a list of the more than 2,000 possessions taken from campers, who were repeatedly searched going to and from the camp, through freedom of information (FOI) request. The Chief Constable of Kent, Michael Fuller, was forced to voluntarily refer a report on the Climate Camp policing at Kingsnorth, to the Independent Police Complaints Panel. This internal inquiry found no evidence of wrongdoing, (as usual) though this would later be overturned by the courts, as we shall see.

This review confirmed that officers had confiscated all manner of items: packets of balloon, tents, washing up liquid, a clown's outfit, camping equipment, UHF connectors, cycle helmets, plastic buckets, bin bags, blankets, soap, banners and leaflets, books, party poppers, nail clippers, and a toy plastic gun. In other words, not items that could be used to blockade power stations. The confiscation of life jackets, inflatable dinghies, paddles, and foot pumps could, however, be understandable. (To stop campers from taking to the river around the Hoo peninsula in Kent.) The confiscation of toilet-building material was a more serious hygiene issue, as it limited sanitary facilities. The need for a helicopter was also questioned.

The legal team would be busy for months after, dealing with complaints following the misuse of the stop/search procedure and the recovery of confiscated possessions. The locals who came to look around did not know what to make of it. 'In this elaborate game with our safe enemies, the law becomes something that we exploit, play with and rely on, as well as mock, oppose and disregard,' as blogger Claire Whitney put it. 'Operation Oasis had radicalised a generation!' In camp, there was a lot of talk about how to build on current 'momentum' and systematically blockade work from then onwards. Clearly, this would attract a smaller and ever-dwindling number of people because of the long-term commitment to direct action necessary, unless substantial local support was forthcoming. *Unfortunately, that had not materialised.* The Midlands barrio alone did an action. The proposed 'rolling blockade' of construction work was to be firmed up over the coming months, talking about blocking the contractors, chaining themselves to construction vehicles and targeting suppliers around the country. Activists from *Don't Build Kingsnorth* invaded the Dartford offices of construction firm *Laing O'Rourke*, one of the bidders for

Kingsnorth Mark 2, Britain's first coal-fired power plant in 30 Years.

The camp did achieve one of its aims: the power station proposal was dropped, following the hiatus over carbon capture. An overwhelming *227 MPs vetoed new coal power* stations without carbon capture. It was exciting but hard-won. Christopher Rootes, (director of the Centre for the Study of Social and Political Movements), was convinced that direct action had played a part. 'I think direct action on aviation and coal was crucial because it managed to move (them) up the agenda in a quite spectacular way. With coal, direct action had an absolutely critical effect in awakening the Government to the contradictions between what it was saying about the need for carbon reductions and its apparent complacency in the face of power industry proposals for new coal-burning power stations (without).'

There were a number of follow-on actions. Ten arrests followed a Greenpeace campaigner swimming ahead of a container ship to try to prevent it from delivering its load of coal down the Medway to Kingsnorth power station. Emma Gibson, from Whitstable, in Kent, said it was worth it to get her voice heard. She had targeted the vessel late on a Sunday night.

She was one of three women who jumped into the water from inflatable speedboats at about 22:50 as it approached the power station near Hoo. 'I was surprised. I thought that it (the ship) would stop when it saw us down there, but it didn't,' she said. 'It just kept on coming and we just realised that the only thing we could do was to get out of the way before we got squashed, basically.'

The coastguard spokesman Colin Ingram said: 'If the master of the vessel had to take evasive action then the vessel could have run aground and we could have ended up with a pollution incident in the Medway, which would have been catastrophic for all the wildlife.' Ships containing large loads could not simply stop on demand, he said. E.On condemned the campaigners' action. Spokesperson Emily Highmore said: 'We need to work together, we need to stop fighting with each other. So talk with us, work with us, don't put yourselves in danger, and don't put our guys in danger.'

On 11 August, six Climate Camp activists clambered onto the roof of the Smithfield meat market to highlight the links between climate change and meat consumption. They dropped a banner bearing the message 'Fight climate change – Go Vegan'.

Meanwhile, in Europe, copycat camps had begun springing up. These were inspired by the UK model in Germany but not organised with such a comprehensive blueprint. The Hamburg theme was twofold: Moorburg (coal) power station and opposition to deportation flights. There were separate press groups and websites. 'Global Social Rights', if inspired by the British model, nevertheless lacked its neighbourhood structure. The target was the site of the proposed 830 MW coal-fired power plant in Moorburg, Hamburg, in 2008, and to burn high-sulphur lignite, without carbon capture.

Further direct action followed in August 2015, at the Hambach opencast mine (which supplied that power station).

Now the expansion of this mine has been deferred, because of a protected species of a bat, a Bechstein, whose habitat it threatened. The company mines an estimated 40 million tonnes of brown coal from the Hambach field annually.

Meanwhile, the Lodge Hill site in Kent is itself now under threat of housing development, despite being an SSSI.

Chapter 14
2009 Camp in the City
(1 May 2009)

Blackheath (27 August – 2 September 2009).

2009 saw several actions over multiple metropolitan locations. Organisers from *Climate Camp, Plane Stupid* and *Climate Rush* launched an online poll, *The Great Climate Swoop*, which was used to pick which coal-fired power station demonstrators should try and close down in a mass swoop on the 17 and 18 October (Ratcliffe).

The two summer camps were in London. 2009's activities...split into two parts, direct action in the City (May), workshops and networking at Blackheath, London (August). The direct action targeting Ratcliffe-on-Soar power station, near Nottingham, was scheduled for mid-October.

This was the first year that no specific target was picked for a summer event. This was a deliberate decision to attract a wider base of support, at Kingsnorth; dependent as it was on anarchic and unpredictable affinity groups.

May Day throughout Europe has long been associated with street protest. In England, this has invariably turned violent. 2009 was to prove no different. The 'spectacular action' at *Camp in the City* in the financial centre of London on that day also coincided with the arrival of global leaders in the UK for the G20 summit in Watford. This drew heavily on the black bloc anarchist element, veterans of many a May Day; and anyway, the police were hardly likely to allow camping on a major street junction in the City.

As one blogger put it: 'Looking up at the buildings around us, we were reminded that this is what the police will protect at any cost, this is what our government will sacrifice our civil liberties for bankers who feed off the world's resources and the world's poorest people; those are the ones who can sleep safely. With the level of media distortion in commentaries on police activities and protest coverage, it is easy to believe that there you cannot expect justice as a protester. If the government sacrifices the welfare of all concerned citizens to play big boys on the international stage, and the police act as they please during such events, then there are no systems in place to protect those who actually want to save the planet's resources. It's worrying that the real value of the government's green agenda and their prioritisation only comes to light when push comes to shove.'

Several thousand demonstrators found themselves penned in (or 'kettled') by the police outside the Carbon Exchange, a broad plaza at the end of Threadneedle Street. The City of London Police's, *Operation Glencoe,* model made no distinction between 'extreme protest groups, organised crime groups or terrorists'. The press portrayed it with headlines such as 'Anarchy Groups Battle For City', showing pictures of windows being smashed by people wearing masks. 'The protest seemed a broad bricolage of causes:' but, unfortunately, a violent one.

A young man waving a red flag allowed that we're not in a revolutionary situation yet, 'but I think we might be soon'; three feet away, a woman holding one end of a banner ('Capitalism isn't working') said she was furious with Gordon Brown for saddling her children with debt and may well vote for the Tories in the next election. But Mary— retired, with a 'Wage Slave' label on—rebuked my cynicism. 'I refute the idea that we're all talking about different things,' she said. 'The kind of world we want to see is the same world – a world where money is used to help people. We're all just talking about different bits of it.'

The Kingsnorth camp had been quite traumatic enough for me; I had a job to return to... I felt so intimidated by the police presence and I knew we were getting somewhere – but where? A question I was unable to answer. Following complaints about policing the previous year, the police presence had been scaled back at Blackheath. A number of affinity groups carried out protests at various city HQs' – for example, the European Carbon Exchange and BP HQ.

The Blackheath camp was the second London camp of the year. The campers 'swooped' from seven city-wide locations at noon on Wednesday 26 August – under Waterloo Bridge; outside BP headquarters in St James's Square; Bank of England, Threadneedle Street; Stratford Tube; Rio Tinto offices, Aldermanbury Square; and Stockwell Tube station. This was all organised on social media.

The chosen site was Dartmouth Field, within view of the City itself and near the River Thames '...The Blackheath Climate Camp was cordoned off by temporary fencing. This was erected by the campers themselves before the tents were pitched. This was not entirely intended to keep the police out, but to secure the camp against the sort of baton-and-shield 'clearance' perpetrated against previous sites.' The police had decided it was Operation Glencoe as far as the City was concerned, but a more relaxed Operation Bentham for Blackheath. In the 19th century, Jeremy Bentham envisaged a prison called a panopticon, in which guards could watch prisoners without them knowing they were being watched. This was an attempt to make prisons and workplaces easier to run. Housed in a circular building in which all cells opened inwards onto a courtyard, everyone could be overseen from one central point; a feature first identified by Foucault.

The heath itself was an inspired choice, associated as it was with the Peasants' Revolt – when Watt Tyler led an uprising against taxes back in 1407. This followed the Battle of Deptford Bridge, during which Cornish rebels had been camped there. So, under Operation Bentham, the police left the Blackheath camp alone. It was reportedly the least stressful of all the camps, resulting in just one arrest by the end, in marked contrast to previous years (see Appendix 1).

Climate Camp circulated a letter to local residents, stating their aim as being to demonstrate and talk about the links between the crisis happening to our climate and the financial crisis of capitalism, which they linked with the City of London. They also invited residents to a public meeting. They would be talking to the council about all matters to do with health, waste, parking, and safety issues. 'All of the camps in previous years have attracted many members of the local community and we hope this year will be no different.' It was good to see health and safety on the radar.

'The event is financed by personal and voluntary donations, participants are encouraged to donate £5 per day

173

for the meals, however, this is not a mandatory levy and people are free to eat without paying.' Erecting a single camera in the nearby Territorial Army car park in Blackheath (the police) joined in a game of rural role-play. They went very '*Dixon of Dock Green*' about the whole enterprise. In general, the atmosphere inside the camp was more relaxed than previous years, and, after a few days, the self-imposed circle of steel, decorated loosely with random anti-globalisation banners, was being questioned by the hard-core 'Black Bloc' anarchists.

The *Anarchist Federation,* however, was less than impressed. This was not their bag: 'The debates and discussions that have been prominent in the neighbourhoods are largely concerned with the anti-social behaviour of campers on-site, *not* our ability to forward our movement. There has even been some approval of allowing the police to enter our autonomous space in the spirit of future "good relations". In truth, the only real political work that has come out of this camp is the "Eco-lobbying" of the media team, aided by media-friendly direct actions on certain key infrastructure.'

At Blackheath camp, introspection was to begin in earnest, with a full day of the discussion focused on 'where next?' A further three-day gathering in Bristol raised 40 different proposals, far too many to deal with at once. The question was why had they stopped growing and how could this be changed? Further meetings continued into 2011, as we shall see in chapter 16.

The police had even extended their welcome to the legal team. 'It really was weird,' said Frances Wright, a member of the Climate Camp legal team: so when, in the build-up to this year's camp, the activists half thought it was a wind-up. 'When you've been charged by the police, when you've had the sort of experiences with them that most of us have had, you get a kind of physical reaction to them, you want to get away from them. So meeting them at Gravesend station and stepping, voluntarily, into a police minivan, in order to be carried off to one of their operation centres, was just really, really surreal.' The police had, inevitably, been on an all-out charm offensive ever since the appalling scenes captured on video at the May G20 protests in the City of London. They had also appointed a woman for the first time as silver commander and engaged far more willingly with activists than hitherto.

However, everyone attending this protest was still photographed by the FIT for their records. In a national opinion poll commissioned by the charity Christian Aid, 33% of people had said that recording protesters was a breach of their privacy, while 18% said they had been intimidated from taking part in environmental protests by police tactics.

The Metropolitan Police set up a Twitter feed through which they communicated with demonstrators…'The force will tweet about issues such as *policing of the camp, info from other emergency services and local community info* at @CO11MetPolice in an attempt to engage protesters.'

Nor the bloggers: 'No mass hijacking, blockading or noisy interruption was penned for execution in the swoop. Were the activists being even more troublesome by not reverting to stereotype?…reporters became increasingly bored by the placid introspective camp.'

Or this one '…the role of activists in Europe (that is, everyone who was actually there for the discussion) was simply to provide verbal solidarity with the Bolivians and South Africans in their fight against capitalism. At the same time, it's hard to imagine anyone who's had to deal with the miserable reality of working-class life for many people in Britain talking about anti-capitalism as if it was simply a process of cheering for the good guys in Asia or South America, and failing to see that any meaningful, effective anti-capitalist movement must be rooted in the struggle to win control over our own lives.'

The worker-occupation of a wind turbine factory under threat of closure in the Isle of Wight was a case in point. 'Seven workers at the Vestas plant in Newport, Isle of Wight, remain inside the building this evening despite Vestas obtaining an eviction order earlier this morning. Four of their colleagues left the plant during the afternoon, deciding to bring their protest to an end so that they could be reunited with friends and families. In a statement read out on their behalf, they thanked everyone for their support.' The occupation was all over in a week, without any involvement from the campers. The closure went ahead. Meanwhile, a large wind turbine facility is being built elsewhere, on the Humber. It had the potential to link the revolutionary anti-capitalist theory with the here and now of people's lives.

The occupation reminded me of more optimistic times four decades before, when a scheme known as 'swords for ploughshares' was being seriously considered by the then Labour Government. 3 600 workers at Lucas Aerospace were threatened with redundancy. The shop stewards combined committee drew up an alternative corporate plan for socially useful and environmentally desirable production. This was a very positive aspect of trade unionism; but was, predictably, rejected by the owners.

Even Lawrence Summers, former US Treasury Secretary and World Bank Chief would agree that 'what is good for the global economy and its business champions' isn't necessarily good for workers.'

Internationally, Argentina was the country with the longest tradition of factory worker occupations. Their economic 2001 crisis had seen factories and businesses closing by the dozen, leaving millions unemployed. Used to being at the rough end of the global economy, many Argentinian workers reclaimed businesses ranging from 5-star hotels and pastry factories to metal works.

In the UK, a solitary action between *Reclaim the Streets* and the Liverpool Dockers – this was '…more the product of mutual weakness and isolation'. What these schemes did have in common was a pre-industrial, communal decision-making process. In a country like Argentina, where 60 percent of people live below the poverty line, reclaiming a factory or business, running it autonomously and horizontally, and everyone getting fair wages was empowering and life fulfilling.

The *National Movement of Recovered Factories* claimed to run 60 factories employing 3600 workers, while the *National Federation of Workers' Cooperatives in Recovered Factories* had 14 factories with 447 workers.

By 2009, the camp model was being copied all over the world (see Appendix 1). Most were generally focused on a particular community polluter, usually with a dirty fossil fuel focus – mining or power stations fired by coal or peat. There was an attempt to close three peat-fired power stations in

County Offaly in Eire (a massive source of CO^2 – one power station had only opened the year before). The contribution of peat marsh to long-term fluctuations in these atmospheric gases has long been a matter of degree. There was an abortive attempt to blockade a railway at Ffos y Fran mine in Wales, back in April 2009, when several members of *Coal Action Scotland* locked on to the tracks in order to stop a train carrying coal to Aberthaw, the dirtiest power station in Wales. Since the 2005 general election, at least 54 new opencast mines have been approved.

Meanwhile, in Scotland, there was the occupation of Mainshill Wood, an opencast coal mine near Douglas, in southern Scotland, a visiting PhD student from the USA, Kirstie Stramler, produced a coal health study to highlight the health impacts of opencast mining.

This action centred on the sabotage of a coal conveyor belt, so this was not NVDA. Running from Glentaggart opencast mine to the Ravenstruther rail terminal responsible for transporting hundreds of tonnes of coal over 7km, this was the UK's longest conveyor. Scottish Coal had been given permission to opencast mine 1.7 million tonnes of coal on land belonging to Lord Home, the chair of Coutts Bank, where the Harpenden wood camp was situated. The proposed mine would come within 1km of the local hospital.

Another protest at an opencast mine in South Wales, the Ffos-y-Fran, failed to happen. Reclaim the Power and Earth First! Were infiltrated by Boyling, the undercover officer. Four members of *Rising Tide* were ordered to pay £10 000 compensation costs to the owners of the mine. Five hundred locals attempted court action in their defence, but their group application was refused by the High Court as they were deemed 'unable to afford it'.

Climate Camp activists had also organised 'flash mobs' at many E.On student recruitment events, given out leaflets at E.On sponsored FA Cup football matches – even disrupted a climate change conference sponsored by them. 'Mass Popular Anti-Recruitment Actions' were co-ordinated by students and activists involved in such groups as *People & Planet,* and *Coal Action Network* in addition to the *Camp for Climate Action*. For example, the entire Cambridge recruitment fair was placed on security alert, protesters had entered the fair donned in red 'E.On off' and yellow 'leave it in the ground' T-shirts and handed out leaflets in dialogue with careers reps under the scrutiny of UkUncut.

University authorities had threatened to remove activists if they leafleted or took pictures/video, so instead, they just talked to careers reps. The reps, in general, seemed taken aback by this, platitudes about 'keeping the lights on', 'commitment to exploring renewable energy' and 'green schemes' like cycle to work schemes. Activists outside unfurled a huge 'make a living, not a killing' banner from a bridge, as well as *CND* and *Cambridge Students Against the Arms Trade* banners lining the path to the fair. They handed out leaflets outside, urging students to vet the companies they might work for, and distributing info about ethical career opportunities. Dr James Hansen came to address the campaigners at the Warwick University one, located just outside the E.On head office, in support of the camp.

E.On threw in the towel and suspended any further recruitment fairs that year. By then seventeen of its career stalls at universities around the country had been disrupted.

Other actions targeted E.On's PR firm *Edelman*, as well as construction firms bidding for the Kingsnorth contract.

Jane Benson of the *Camp for Climate Action* said: 'This is a great step for the campaign against a new coal-fired power station at Kingsnorth. E.On know, they can't defend their plans in the midst of a climate crisis. So, rather than be embarrassed in front of potential employees, they've chosen to run away.'

On 19 June, Campers and 40 members of *Rising Tide* organised a Greenwash Guerrillas demo outside the *UK Guardian Climate Change Summit*. This was another E.On sponsored event at the Business Design Centre in Islington. Protected by toxic waste hazard suits and brandishing a top-of-the-line range of 'Greenwash detecting devices', the 40 intrepid Greenwash Guerrillas swarmed around the building.

What may be said was that the camp in the city acted as the template for the *Occupy St Pauls* movement in 2011. That is another story.

Chapter 15

Legal Issues of Policing the Camps

The policing of the camps reached its most punitive at the City of London, a step-change up from Kingsnorth the previous year. It would be facile to see the purpose of policing as violently maintaining an oppressive social order. To quote Paul Mobbs:

'The problem we face today is that the objective reality of our situation, both within UK society and as a global community, is not reflected in the public dialogue we see in mainstream politics and the media. There are a number of serious issues related to the values that form the heart of the present political and economic consensus that portends a major shift in society. Be it climate change, resource depletion, or the growing disparity between rich and poor, there are a whole range of issues where mainstream politics cannot fully engage in a dialogue because it would invalidate their own present ideological position. For this reason, suppression of the debate becomes the *least damaging option* within official policy. Police procedures occasionally have to be modified to accord with the European Court of Human Rights.'

'Consequently, this means that to be an extremist you don't have to do anything, you just have to disagree with the views of those in authority. Within the terms of new anti-terrorism laws, action is not even required – you merely need to publicly believe what you say. Therefore, the purpose of these policies is skewed toward not so much the physical well-being of the public, but specifically protecting the present political and economic consensus which they represent.'

So the 'charge' of 'domestic extremist' has been created by the police themselves, not parliament or the courts. According to a senior officer: 'There are lots of reasons why people might be on the (*crimint*) database. Not everyone on there is a criminal and not everyone on there is a domestic extremist, but we have got to build up a picture of *what is happening. Those people may be able to help us in the future.* It's an intelligence database, not an evidence database. Protesting is not a criminal offence but there is occasionally a line that is crossed when people commit offences.'

ACPO's 'Adapting to protest' acknowledges that police officers were not allowed to use $44 of the Criminal Justice Act indiscriminately to randomly search individuals. They must instead use $43, which requires a reason. This law was broken at Kingsnorth, where the court ruled that $44 was being used as a form of harassment. 'The danger is that by using surveillance to frustrate a minority, the police deter a huge, moderate coalition of people from peaceful civic participation,' according to Daleep Mukarji, the Director of *Christian Aid*.

Overt police surveillance tactics at Kingsnorth—carried out by their forward intelligence team (FIT)—were praised in a National Policing Improvement Agency report' The FIT would tend to withdraw if challenged by a crowd, especially if photographed.

'My guess is that it pushes uncomfortable buttons when we are coping with the messy reality of today by trying to live respectfully with the status quo in the ethos that more of the same, plus some subtle tweaks will be enough to keep us on track. We want to believe that these protest efforts are in vain because it means that inactivity is as effective as activity.' Climate camp had overstepped that with ease. It was what the SDS would term 'bandit country'.

The *Territorial Support group* (Metropolitan police) was the successor body to the *Special Demonstration squad.* They were brought in from Heathrow onwards as the camp moved in the direction of the capital. This is a seriously militarised Kevlar-armoured unit, battens and body-shielded. They were formed in 1968 after anti-Vietnam war protests turned violent in Grosvenor Square outside the US embassy in London. The unprecedented level of violence directed at the police there caused a sea change in training; and response. It was a wake-up call to senior officers in the Metropolitan police who realised they needed a new way to gather intelligence about the hate-filled 'subversives' they now had to deal with.

Undercover agents were given new identities, flats, vehicles and 'cover' jobs while working in the field for years at a time. The person that seeks to discredit or harm another by provoking them to commit a wrong or rash action. Reading the original, much-redacted manual for the SDS is a chilling experience. It gives a fascinating '…insight into the different techniques used to set up and live a false identity and ploys used to deal with situations which may arise'.

Similar measures were taken in the USA. 'Fusion Centres' serve as focal points within the state and local environment for the receipt, analysis, gathering, and sharing of threat-related information between the federal government and state, local, tribal, territorial, and private sector partners. Located in states and major urban areas throughout the USA, these 'umbrella' organisations co-ordinate front-line law enforcement, public safety, fire service, emergency response, public health and private sector security. It also oversaw the infiltration of subversive groups to better protect their communities.

In the USA, sting operations are routinely used to deal with anarchist organisations. 'The FBI has in recent years used trained informants not just to snitch on suspected terrorists, but to frame them. A recent report put together by *Mother Jones* and the Investigative Reporting Program at the University of California-Berkley analyses some striking statistics about the role of FBI informants in terrorism cases that the Bureau has targeted in the decade since the 11 September attacks. The report reveals that the FBI regularly infiltrates communities where they suspect terrorist-minded individuals to be engaging with others.'

UK Police command structure is markedly hierarchical – Strategic, tactical and operational. (Gold, silver and bronze). The philosophy adopted at each event did, however, evolve. By Heathrow, we were on (*Harmony 2)*, at Kingsnorth on (*Operation Oasis*), and then on (*Glencoe*) and (*Bentham)* by Camp in the City and Blackheath, respectively. *Gold* sets tactical parameters but not tactics, which are set by *Silver*. *Bronze* implements the silver strategy – and this is a trained system. At Kingsnorth, it seemed to break down, when the silver command changed their plan during the event, from allowing the peaceful protest to declaring it an illegal one, with the intention to commit damage. In relation to stop and search, this led to a vicious circle of escalation. 'They did not follow the CMM code of practice'.

'The left's traditional view that the police are just the arm of the state is now far too simplistic. The past decade has seen the police emerge as powerful political players in their own right. They are as innately conservative and as ready to use physical force as ever but more influential, more independent and more difficult to hold to account – a kind of Fifth Estate that is almost impossible to reform.' It has now become a moral guardian, something Coronavirus is bound to accelerate. Legislation *The Police, Crime, Sentencing and Courts Bill*, which will be debated by MPs

They are happy with a march from A to B; even *Stop the War* did not threaten the status quo (despite a one-off demo by millions in the streets). The innovative tactics at the Climate Camp, like the anti-roads movement, were a different story. In order to react, police needed intelligence, both within the camp and to pinpoint who they took to be key individuals because legislation targets individuals.

A flat organisational structure like the camp is problematic for police, who need to identify 'key' organisers. An issue which they dealt with by embedding undercover officers on the ground, plus deploying the 'Forward Intelligence team', or FIT. Activists found themselves labelled 'domestic extremists' with their own file on the FIT database. Their photographs were used to match attendees against a database. While the original remit of the FIT may have been to monitor the activities of football hooligans it would be fair to say issues of 'mission creep' and accountability had crept into what they are allowed to do. They need to justify their jobs and keep busy, and this is the easiest way to show results, by placing folks on regular surveillance and harassment schedules of differing periods, depending on the case. They had even been known to accompany activists away from demos – following them to their workplace or homes, on public transport, or tailing their cars as they drove home.

On location, 'capture cards', (some of which had been dropped), were used by the police to match wanted individuals. From the police point of view, they wanted to identify the organisers of the camp, who alone could be charged. Surveillance is, however, a two-way street and *Fitwatch* was the counterpart group formed to photograph and identify police FIT personnel. This highlighted another identity problem. 'Scotland Yard was at the centre of a political row today over officers covering up their lapel numbers. A number of officers are openly defying direct orders by Met Commissioner Sir Paul Stephenson to display the number on their uniforms. Among them is the police sergeant suspended after he was caught on camera with his epaulette covered while attacking protester Nicky Fisher in the wake of the G20 demonstrations. A series of pictures show uniformed officers breaching rules (that) state...they should be 'identifiable at all times.' The Metropolitan police have since purchased embroidered numerals so these will not become dislodged as easily. *Fitwatch* had already made a diagram showing how anyone with a video camera could document a police raid, complete with instructions on angles and height.

In the nineteenth century, Jeremy Bentham envisaged a unique new design of the prison, which he termed a 'panopticon'. Guards would watch prisoners without them knowing they were being watched. If prisoners were housed in a building in which all cells opened inwards onto a courtyard, then everyone could be viewed from one central observation tower. Though the inmates cannot see what goes on in the tower, they know they may be under observation at any given moment, so they come to internalise the surveillance and control themselves. In other words, 'power sees without looking, while the observed look without seeing'. This trend is continuing. The first workhouse at Southwell, east of Nottingham, was the first to put this into practice in the 19thC. It effectively marks the start of the surveillance society in Britain and his panopticon concept. Jeremy Bentham adopted this as the method of control for workhouses or prisons. This model was adopted all over the world. It certainly influenced the Metropolitan police, who went as far as to borrow the strategy for the 2009 camp – 'Operation Bentham'. One camera overviewed the site. The name says it all!

Writing in the *Guardian*, the journalist John Lanchester had this to say: '…we risk becoming: a society which is in crucial respects a giant panopticon, where the people with access to our secrets can see, hear, intercept and monitor everything'. 'What this adds up to today is a new thing in human history: with a couple of clicks of a mouse, an agent of the state can target your home phone, or your mobile, or your email, or your passport number, or any of your credit card numbers, or your address, or any of your logins to a web service; a database of photos.' In a national opinion poll commissioned by the charity *Christian Aid*, 33% of people felt that recording of protesters was a breach of their privacy, while 18% said they had been put off going to environmental protests by police photography. Scotland Yard titled photography as 'isolated incidents' as per usual. Yet that had been going for decades.

The National Extremism Tactical Co-ordination Unit (*NETCU*) was the police team directing the fight against extremists. Their website carries images of people marching with banners, of peace campaigners standing outside a military base, and even of the *Clandestine Insurgent Rebel Clown Army* (*CIRCA*) whose members dress up as clowns to show their peaceful intentions; it had been particularly successful in infiltrating the *Animal Liberation Front*. By 2004, it had pretty much dismantled the animal rights movement, the offence of 'economic damage' which saw one activist jailed for 4.5 years for holding a banner and updating a website.

Even the Clown army was a target. What threat could they have been? Their undercover clown was Officer 'A' – known as Lynn Watson, from Leeds. The (former) website stated: 'We are clandestine because we refuse the spectacle of celebrity, and without real names, faces or noses, we show that our words, dreams, and desires are more important than our biographies. We are insurgents because we have risen up from nowhere and are everywhere and because an insurrection of the imagination is irresistible. We are rebels because we love life and happiness more than 'revolution' and because while no revolution is ever complete, rebellions continue forever. We are clowns because inside everyone is a lawless clown trying to escape, and because nothing undermines authority like holding it up to ridicule. We are an army because we live on a planet in permanent war – a war of money against life, of profit against dignity, of progress against the future. We are an army because a war that gorges itself on death and blood and shits money and toxins deserve an obscene body of deviant soldiers. We are clowns because we are approximate and ambivalent, neither here nor there, but in the most powerful of all places, the place in-between order and chaos.' Dangerous stuff!

The Forward Intelligence Unit (*FIT*) continued to stake out London planning meetings. They were filming everyone going in and out. From the NECTU website: 'Details of individuals are recorded because they are witnesses to acts of criminality or anti-social behaviour. The information recorded is used to identify those who have committed criminal acts and to eliminate from enquires, those *who are not at fault.* Simply recording a person's details does not imply that the individual is guilty of incidents of criminality. 'If an individual has their details recorded on several occasions this is likely to be because those individuals have attended several events where violent disorder has occurred.' Is this intimidation? I certainly avoided one meeting when I saw them outside the squat venue.

What is of more concern to activists is that (*NETCU's*) role is to liaise with, advise and support corporations and private companies that have become '*victims*' of protest campaigns Concerns that *NETCU* has shared police intelligence with these companies and stepped well beyond supposed neutrality. It is argued that 'economic damage' is an imprisonable offence.

Another of its specialities was misleading press releases. In November 2008, a 'senior source' *NETCU* said it had growing evidence of a threat from eco-activists. 'We have found statements that four-fifths of the human population has to die for other species in the world to survive.' This concern is related to an entry on the *Earth First!* Website. Officers were '…concerned a "lone maverick" eco-extremist might attempt a terrorist attack aimed at killing large numbers of Britons…' there are a number of very dedicated individuals out there and they could be dangerous to other people. Since then we have witnessed a pandemic, which has killed as many people as die in a war. Far more of a problem. I've always hoped that I was immune to experiments like this (including the Milgram experiment and Das Experiment), but who knows what evil is hidden in all of us?

Home office minister, Nick Herbert was concerned about accountability, stating '…units like this should not be operated by *ACPO* and they should be operated either by a lead police force or in future, the *National Crime Agency* where there is proper governance in place.' By summer 2011, it passed into the control of the Metropolitan Police, with a budget of £8 million a year, it is too early to draw any conclusions as to what will change as a result of this proposal. There is a guidance manual, a code of practice on Undercover Policing, published by the College of Policing. This describes the process of 'legend building', the faking of an identity. UCOs are expected to be conversant with legislation and practices that will have an impact on 'legend building'. Activists have documented the range of counter-techniques used in their own manual.

The publicity surrounding the Mark Kennedy affair has in fact revitalised the activist cause. Damaging allegations, including perjury and tacit consent, continue to be raised. On January 13, it was revealed that a second, female, undercover 'Officer A' (nom de plume Lyn Watson) had been active in Leeds since 2004 – undercover in the Clown Army and trustee of the Common Place social centre. She allowed herself to be arrested for gluing herself to the Department for Transport, as part of the Heathrow protest in February 2008.

'Lyn Watson' attempted to justify herself: 'What we have seen is ill-informed communication about our actions', a message intended to suggest that confusion over police tactics, rather than outright duplicity, was the reason why the Metropolitan Police has faced criticism. Assistant Commissioner Owens said that (senior officers have a)...' leadership responsibility to prevent a locker room mentality' among officers. If only this really meant something in practice. From G20 and the death of Ian Tomlinson to Gaza and student demonstrations, senior officers have repeatedly failed to shoulder responsibility for the conduct of their officers.

At the same time, and fourteen years of court cases later, the introduction of the *Human Rights Act* in 1998 had failed to mitigate the introduction of this new repressive 'total policing' model. It has instead depended on individuals taking the time, effort (and often crippling expense) of seeking legal redress after their rights have been denied, usually securing no more than the odd civil claim without an admission of liability. Inevitably, it has also often taken the struggle for an end to police misconduct away from campaigners and handed it to lawyers and judges.

Under both $44 of the *Terrorism Act* and $60 of the *Criminal Justice Act*, police had powers to stop and search – but not the right to probe for name and address. By the time we got to Kingsnorth in 2008, this became routine; quite a few thought they were obliged to give their name and address. According to the *Metropolitan Police website*:

> $60 Criminal Justice and Public Order Act 1994, gives police the right to search people in a defined area at a specific time, with the qualification that there is the possibility of *serious violence*; or that they believe a person is carrying a dangerous object or offensive weapon; or that an incident involving serious violence has taken place and a dangerous instrument or offensive weapon used in the incident is being carried in the locality. This law has historically been used *mainly to tackle football hooliganism and gang fights.*'
>
> Another section deals with stopping and searching any vehicle, the vehicle, its driver and any passenger for offensive weapons or dangerous instruments, whether or not there are grounds for suspicion. If they had used $50 of the *Police Reform Act*, they would have the power to arrest for withholding name.

Heathrow had not seen such behaviour. The year after, quite a lot of equipment needed to run the site was confiscated (see Kingsnorth chapter). The police decision to deploy batons and shields at Kingsnorth was met with widespread ridicule, as the camp was three miles away from the power station, and the adoption of the total policing model seemed less about protecting the target than routing the camp. Even the police review queried the need for a helicopter.

'In addition, a number of autonomous social centres which have been used by the movement, have since had problems with licensing. The Common Place (Leeds) lost both their performance and alcohol license following the showing of a film dealing with police violence. 'Lyn Watson' (officer A) was a founding trustee. Some like the *Common Place*, are rented, some squatted, and some cooperatively owned. They describe themselves as 'autonomous' to stress that they do it themselves, without help. *'Common Place* did not get their license replaced until 7 September 2009, but three weeks later, the court decided that they would be liable for the legal costs of their appeal: £15 000. It would have required substantial commitment from volunteers to help pay, as *Common Place* was a 'not for profit' enterprise. At a special AGM in January 2010 they called it a day; the negative feelings about the building were clear; it was described as a dark, unfriendly space. Her use of a false name (known as *ledgending*) was a factor too. *The UCO had fulfilled her brief.*

The HMIC review had been expected to highlight a failure of supervision and suggest police chiefs ensured officers were not left on undercover assignments for 'too long' in the future. *It did not take that opportunity.* The average was six years. *But it did not call for judges, rather than police chiefs, to authorise undercover operations, which would have put some balance into the equation...*

'Of the seven undercover police officers so far identified as having infiltrated protest groups, five had sexual relationships as part of their cover, often developing long-term relationships and fathering children. They include Lambert, Boyling and Black, as well as Mark Kennedy, who was unmasked as a police spy last year.' In Lambert's case, a son is seeking compensation from the Met. At least *thirty-five women* have been deceived into relationships.

At a meeting at the London Anarchist Bookfair, those who'd known Mark revealed that he had been active in ecological, animal rights, anti-fascist and anti-capitalist movements. He was involved in setting up the direct action camp in Stirling during the G8 protests of 2005 and the first Climate Camp, amongst other things. He was also implicated in linking with activists across Europe and, possibly, even in the USA.

The Crown Prosecution Service had ruled (22 August 2014) that '…there was insufficient evidence' to prosecute the four officers involved for offences including rape, indecent assault and misconduct in public office. A civil lawsuit, on behalf of at least ten women, however, was successfully settled out of court in 2016.

On 16 July 2015, Theresa May, the then Home Secretary, announced a public inquiry into undercover policing since 1968. This was named after Justice Mitting. This decision followed further revelations that police officers had used the names of dead children to create their new identities, which was met with abhorrence ('legend building'). They had also had long-term, intimate relationships with women, fathered children, committed perjury and in some cases acted as agent provocateurs. This inquiry (Mitting) will eventually be made public. To quote the judge: 'It seems likely that the Inquiry will expose both creditable and discreditable conduct, practice and management. As far as I am aware, this is the first time that undercover policing has been exposed to the rigour of public examination.' The public inquiry received over one million pages from the Metropolitan Police Service alone. The public hearing has yet to sit. Criminal offences such as destroying evidence created by $35 of the *Inquiries Act 2005* apply only to conduct 'during the course of any inquiry'. These allegations pre-date its existence. It was announced recently that it is not due to finish until 2023, much to the disgust of the women who wanted their day in court.

One of the definitive issues to be covered by the Mitting inquiry will be if deployments prevented, detected, or helped the prosecution of crime. So far, more than 64 undercover police officers have had their cover names published; and over a thousand groups or organisations are referred to in Special Demonstration Squad documentation.

After a statement has been received from an individual officer, the Inquiry intends that requests for evidence be made both from those managing or responsible for the officer and from non-state individuals affected by or during the deployment. The timescale is extensive and the end date of 2023 is envisaged.

'It is institutional, political and endemic abuse concealed within our 'society'. The established principle, of neither confirm nor deny (NCND) used by law enforcement agencies protects covert methods, sensitive information and the identity of sources of information, including Undercover Offices. 'NCND' is not used to hide information that the force or agency wishes to hide. Rather, it safeguards tactics and the lives and well-being of Undercover Officers, their families and others. 'Sometimes simply confirming or denying whether a force or agency holds a particular category of information could itself disclose sensitive and damaging information.' The principle of NCND, the police said, was needed to prevent harm that may arise if law enforcement agencies hold particular information. Specifically: to confirm that a person is an undercover officer would place that person in immediate and obvious danger; to deny that a person is a UCO may place another person in immediate and obvious danger to comment either way in one case raises a clear inference where there is a refusal to comment in another case that there is something to hide in that case. A liaison role amongst SDS officers was protected by the Met, who sought to withhold the identity.

The police can recruit informers. Their attempt to recruit a *Plane Stupid* supporter backfired. Tilly Gifford documented her recruitment in a social media post. The financial inducement was recorded by her on a hidden camera in Scotland. She posted it on YouTube, and it was featured on the *Guardian* website. The Home Office has failed to extend the enquiry into Scotland, nor has the Scottish Government set up its own public inquiry into #*spycops*. Tilly took the government to Court for this omission. Her case was thrown out.

Then on 30 August that year, the existence of undercover 'Officer B' was revealed to be Marco Jacobs, real name again withheld amid fears for his safety in other operations. I believe I met him once at a planning meeting; he had previously been working undercover for four years, infiltrating an anarchist group in Cardiff.

We did witness, during the G8 Summit at Gleneagles in 2005, the Metropolitan Police send undercover police officers across the border. In addition, English undercover officers also had intimate relations with a number of women they targeted in Scotland, a repeated human rights violation that the Metropolitan Police Service has publicly apologised for. The UK Government refused to extend the terms of reference of the Undercover Policing Inquiry to cover Scotland, under and in terms of the Inquiries Act of 2005. But Tilly nevertheless left that role.

"Kettling" is the preferred strategy of encirclement to corral and contain people as used by the Met. 'The term "kettle" is rather apt, given that penning already outraged people into a small space tends to make tempers boil and give the police an excuse to turn up the heat, and it doesn't take long for that to happen.' Kettling sits uncomfortably with Articles 10 and 11 of the *Human Rights Act*, which permits dissent. It does not easily allow the release of peaceful protesters from confinement, a fact now recognised by HMIC in *Adapting to Protest*, recommendation 11. The courts seem uncertain about the legality of kettling in every situation. Case law goes back to 2001, in Metropolitan Police Commissioner (2009) AC 564, (2009) 3 All ER 455.

The tactics used at 2009's Climate Camp in the City were illegal, the High Court ruled. 'Sir Anthony May, President of the Queen's Bench Division, and Mr Justice Sweeney ruled. On review, the policing of the Climate Camp demonstration outside the European Carbon Exchange during the 2009 G20 summit was criticised. The kettling of some 4000 or 5000 demonstrators for almost five hours was ruled unlawful. 'Unnecessary' and 'unjustified' force was used to drive the crowd 30 metres back, including offensive 'shield strikes'. Instructions to subordinate officers were, they said, '…not satisfactory, very general and imprecise'. During the course of the evening, 'officers declined to release people who should have been released.' Police evidence given that campers were intent on disorder and criminality by the senior officer responsible for the operation, CI Johnson, was 'not…convincing.'

Liberty contended police used *kettling* to their advantage. Police tactics included pushing and slapping demonstrators and using shields as weapons. This is well documented on video. 'The possibility of mass containment of peaceful protesters has undoubtedly had a chilling effect on many people's rights to freedom of expression and assembly. 'What is needed is a technique to actually weed out the guilty from the innocent.'

A further test case was brought by Josh Moos and Hannah McClure, two out of several thousand demonstrators (and Bindman's clients) that had gathered outside the Carbon Exchange on the eve of the G20 summit. The purpose of that demonstration was to draw attention to the trading scheme's failure to address the underlying causes of climate change. They were kettled without warning at just after 7 pm and held until shortly after midnight, after which they and others who had wanted to camp overnight were driven away. 'The Divisional Court considered that lawful.'

The High Court was in two minds. A single image can often seem iconic. Kettling is a photogenic spectacle created by the state. Some of those suing had suffered physical injury or were deprived of access to medical attention, raising questions of proportionality. It ruled that, while the kettle could not be justified when it was first imposed at 7.07 pm, it *could* have been later in the evening to seal off side roads and impose a cordon to the north of the camp. Two judges added that they were 'not persuaded' a pushing operation against a 15-person deep crowd was 'reasonably necessary.'

Finally, a claimant in 'Austin' sought to take her case to the *European Court of Human Rights*. The verdict '…had been hailed as a victory for civil rights campaigners and the protest movement in general. But this turned out to be premature, as the verdict was then *reversed on appeal* in January 2012. Now the defendants, (like the Common Place social centre before them) faced financial ruin: heavy legal costs were awarded against them. The Appeal Court held that kettling…' was justifiable on the ground, that containment was the *least drastic* way of preventing a breach of the peace. The new verdict gave the benefit of doubt to the police; the Met has subsequently reaffirmed its commitment to using the tactic where it is considered to be necessary. So it may well continue for the foreseeable future; it was not long before it was used again. There should be less need for sudden unlawful imprisonment of demonstrators if conditions were better managed.

The pressure group *Liberty* had 120 observers for the TUC march on 26 March. Two of them were allowed inside Scotland Yard's Special Operations Room (SOR). 'They noted that kettling was…under near-constant consideration when potential trouble emerged. Those planning to sue the police following recent events have complained that 'kettling is now the *only trick in the police locker*'. Those suing will be seeking disclosure of police documents to scrutinise whether the kettling was pre-planned; if it was, this may undermine any police contention that the tactic was used to prevent an imminent threat to public order.

In Europe, it is clear that the policing model is less consensual. The Danish police clearly planned 'pre-crime' mass arrests at the Copenhagen COP summit. The Danish government had given them tougher new powers, the infamous 'lømmelpakken' ('hooligan pack'). During the summit's first days, in its newspaper, the police were allowed to make a 'preventive' arrest of a person even if he had not done anything (*Rätvisepartiet Socialisterna*.) He can then be held for up to twelve hours. 'If they get officially arrested, the police may hold a foreign person for 72 hours without a court order. All of Copenhagen had been made a check point zone.'

On the pre-emptive raid on climate change campaigners at Ratcliffe: 'nobody has the right to break the law'. But what if one law contradicts another? How are the courts supposed to resolve that? We shall see this in the next chapter.

Chapter 16
Ratcliffe-On-Soar Power Station (October 2009)

This was the police sting that resulted in the arrest of all concerned in advance of the action. It was the 'pre-crime' high noon of the movement. I understand that the choice, E.On's Ratcliffe plant on the River Soar, was made in January 2009, following an internet poll to choose between either Drax or Ratcliffe. The power plant, which lies eight miles southwest of Nottingham, had previously seen protests by environmental campaigners, including members of *Eastside Climate Action* from Nottingham.

Now we know that (undercover) Mark Kennedy gave the campers his opinion on the best way to break into the plant, then passed this information to his supervisor; ironic indeed as the lead agent provocateur. Over the preceding few months, there is even evidence that Kennedy funded the planned break-in, acquiring tat, presumably using public money and hiring a van under his fake identity. Entrapment would be proven if the idea of committing the crime came from the police, rather than the defendant. If so, then the issue of entrapment identified by the High Court is relevant. He had by then (unknown to his friends) set up *Tokra Ltd*, a private Security Company, at the same address as a security firm, which works for the energy company E.On.

This E.On power station was the largest CO^2 source in the Midlands (7.8 million tonnes every year). The conviction of the 'Ratcliffe 20' was, however, overturned in July 2011, as will be described. All the time, Kennedy was feeding inside information back to his handlers at the National Public Order Intelligence Unit (NPOIU). On 7 April 2009, 'as intelligence from the undercover officer increased', a senior Nottingham police officer authorised Kennedy to use 'audio recording equipment' to record organising meetings. It was subsequently revealed this was a custom-made £7000 wristwatch with a mike and memory chip. It all became a bit, John Le Carre! The appeal court judges said they shared the 'great deal of justifiable public disquiet' about the case, hinging on withholding of evidence by the prosecution counsel.

The Lord Chief Justice said that 'elementary principles' of a fair trial process had been ignored when prosecutors glossed over Kennedy's role to defence lawyers. This was a damning indictment. The *IPCC* watchdog blamed this on a 'communication breakdown' between *NECTU* and the *CPS*. The Police defended their decision to arrest 114 environmental campaigners prior to protest at a power station, on the grounds of conspiracy. The charge was unusual in so far as it had never been used before; 'Conspiracy to Commit Aggravated Trespass'. 'Our information was that it wasn't to be a lawful protest. This was to be a criminal act against a power station. Had that taken place, we would have now been policing a major protest at a major power station.' The men and women were held in (Iona school), Sneinton Dale, Nottingham, on Monday and later released on bail. Police maintained that they had been planning to cause 'prolonged disruption' at the Ratcliffe-On-Soar power station. This was more or less correct as the core had hoped to shut the power station for 7 days.

E.On had already warned its staff about possible protests. In a letter sent to around 17,000 staff employed nationally, the company's chief executive told them that protesters had already tried to shut down power stations and get access to the firm's offices. The accompanying leaflet offered personal safety advice on how to handle possible encounters with protesters.

More than 200 officers from Nottinghamshire, Derbyshire, Leicestershire, Staffordshire and British Transport Police took part in the raid at the Iona School in Sneinton shortly after midnight – at a reported cost of £300,000. Considerable damage was done to the school entrance, though no resistance had been offered. Superintendent Mike Manley of Nottinghamshire Police said large amounts of equipment had been found, including '...food and various devices used for climbing, cutting and locking on to machinery'. He said: 'We think it was a sophisticated attempt to disrupt what we now believe was Ratcliffe-on-Soar Power Station...'

The hold-up of a Drax coal train the previous year had, by contrast, only resulted in four arrests. (The power station could use 36,000 tonnes of coal a day). The school board was upset; the campers too. Nor did police offer to repair the damage they caused to the School, which was unable to open were trespassing. A classic sting (codenamed *Operation*

Aeroscope) was used to target the land group; officers knew that *some* of those arrested 'had links' to climate change groups, which had protested at Kingsnorth power station in Kent, Heathrow Airport and Drax power station in North Yorkshire – but none of these were deemed illegal. Following another action at Ratcliffe power station, Nottingham South MP Alan Simpson raised concerns over the nature of the policing operation. 'The scale of it makes people think we are dealing with a major terrorist incident,' he said.

David Porter, chief executive of the *Association of Electricity Producers*, condemned the campaigners' call to stop burning fossil fuels. 'If you suddenly close down our power stations that would be a suicidal policy. The economy of the UK would be seriously disrupted. And there would be social implications of that. It's a nonsensical approach to the problem.'

There were no reported injuries and local residents reported that handcuffed suspects '...sang loudly as they were led away.' In January 2011, the Nottinghamshire police had realised that 'significant' media coverage followed the collapse of the trial was damaging to consensual policing. They referred their pre-emptive action to the IPCC. Their report did not appear until February 2012. This found that the Crown Prosecution Service had failed to read all the documents they had been given. By virtue of $78 of the *Police and Criminal Evidence Act 1984*, a Judge may take into account the circumstances in which evidence was obtained in considering the adverse effect on the fitness of proceeding, and had taken that option.

The Home Secretary was broadly supportive – Alan Johnson said: 'All public authorities must start from a position supporting those who want to exercise their right to peaceful protest. The public can expect some inconvenience and nuisance as a consequence of the state upholding those rights. This is a hallmark of an open, democratic society.' Mr Johnson added the policing of future protests should adopt 'community-style' tactics. He said: 'This means no surprises of policing. It means, better information for protesters and local communities about the policing approach.'

A lawyer representing 26 of the accused stated: 'The State is systematically trying to disrupt young campaigners, taking the only action they can on issues which are vital for future generations – like climate change and social justice. The prosecution (has) said nothing about how the material came not to be disclosed to the defence. It is significant that this development comes from the CPS. The police— Nottinghamshire police, the National Public Order Intelligence, the Metropolitan Police, and ACPO—remain tight-lipped.'

We now know that the decision to drop prosecution hinged on non-disclosure to the prosecution of audio recording on the UCO's wristwatch, a recording that would have supported the defence argument that not all defendants were unanimous. A tape that was never listened to by the CPS. Another unanswered question is: How is the state funding the hire vehicle to transport equipment to the power station 'not encouraging others'?

'The prosecution (has) not even purported to address the wider serious questions of the principle and policies and compliance with policies surrounding the use of undercover police against protest movements, not just climate campaigners on this occasion. Perhaps above all, the impression remains that the Establishment has sought to undermine those campaigning against the urgent and extreme perils of climate change and, once discovered, grudgingly are conceding only as much as they have to, when they have to.' The police's reluctance to reveal their methods had failed to impress the Judiciary.

I did recognise some of the UCO's concerns now, that some identities have been published but had never previously suspected them. I had been suspicious at one time about someone who seemed too well dressed, and whose cover story (reformed accountant) seemed implausible. According to the *Undercover Research Group,* 'If you have suspicions about a person who is or was in your group, then you should recognise that the chances are you'll never know whether or not those suspicions are groundless.'

I never saw him again. When I mentioned this to a few people there, they replied they had expected there would be infiltration by the police.

By contrast, Jim Boyling was authorised to use his alias even when under oath in court. He affirmed under oath his name and address. Still, under oath, he then gave evidence, under questioning from barristers, to attempt to clear himself and seven other campaigners accused of disorderly behaviour during a demonstration. He told the court he had wanted to unfurl a banner from the window of a government building to promote their cause.

'Jim Sutton', aka the police officer Jim Boyling, had committed perjury. Furthermore, his 'handlers' had conspired to pervert the course of justice. The trial would have been very different in outcome had the magistrates known the truth.

Like Jim, Marco had prior direct action experience. In 2007, having managed to get himself included in the planning process for an action against the LNG (liquid natural gas) pipeline terminal at Milford Haven in west Wales, he was then able to pass information back to the local police that resulted in the arrests of a number of his fellow activists. Though all the criminal prosecutions ultimately collapsed, it was not before the police had raided houses, including Marco's own flat, and obtained computers, in what seems to have been a massive 'fishing expedition'.

Pete Black, who worked alongside Boyling in the covert unit monitoring political campaigners, admitted to the *Guardian* that undercover operatives were *often* prosecuted under their fake identities, as it helped to foster their credibility as genuine campaigners. Two inquiries have yet to report on responsibility for suppressing evidence. The suspicion remains that 'handlers' may have sanctioned perjury (October 2011). This is a very serious criminal offence, and it will be interesting to see how this develops at the public inquiry.

Now a 'defence based on necessity' is to be disallowed. It had been the one used by Greenpeace activists following their occupation of Kingsnorth power station in 2008. The Court of Appeal has since ruled that acts must now be considered in the context of a 'functioning state in which legal disputes can be peacefully submitted to the courts and disputes over what should be law or government policy can be submitted to the arbitrament of the democratic process'. This would preclude that defence.

Chapter 17

Fracking and Oil Tar Sands the Last Gasp of the Petrolheads

Had the camp continued, it is pretty certain it would have taken on *fracking* – in a field on the Fylde estuary in 2010? *Camp Frack* was, in many ways, a copycat operation. The need to invest in renewables was never likely to be easy when such extensive gas resources come to light. According to the British Geological Survey, (2013) the Bowland Shales could contain between 822 trillion cubic feet (tcf) and 2281 tcf, with a central estimate of 1329 tcf. However, whatever the size of the resource, the proportion that can be recovered is merely guesswork. A number of minor earthquakes in the Blackpool area are linked to the exploratory work there; and the postponement of further exploration.

'Fracking' refers to a process of hydraulic fracturing of the ground and involves the injection of pressurised chemicals that create new pathways to recover gas (and oil alike) from the rock. Environmental problems are a likely concern in the UK for shale gas fracturing completions…in shale gas…up to a million gallons of water, plus acid-treated in various ways with (ceramic) proppants and resin-coated sands and other chemicals will probably be required initially to fracture the shale and hold the fractures open.

This was the turning point for a long-established NGO to get involved in the camp scene. This event stirred strong local opposition to Cuadrilla when a weekend protest camp was held near the drilling rig. It has its own website too: nofrackinguk.com (now defunct). The Campaign against Climate Change promoted the weekend anti-shale camp – they called it Camp Frack. This was fronted by Phil Thornhill, mentioned earlier. *Campaign against Climate Change* was an established organiser known for orderly winter marches through London, as well as conferences about climate change.

Until 2011 there were two official bodies who might have carried out an independent review of Government policy on unconventional gas and oil in the public interest – the Royal Commission on Environmental Pollution and the Sustainable Development Commission. Both of them were abolished in 2011, as part of the bonfire of regulation.

In 2010, Cuadrilla Resources had begun drilling exploratory bores into the rock at Preese Hall near Blackpool in northwest England, to begin the UK's first experiments with extracting gas trapped in shale formations. Other companies are drilling in Kent. Cuadrilla claimed that at least five trillion cubic metres were recoverable. Tremors in Blackpool (1 on the Richter scale) were too weak to cause any damage, but they continued throughout 2019. Weak, yes, but nonetheless linked to fracking. It was claimed that there has also been an increase in water pipe fractures.

'Drilling close to urban areas has posed problems, even for conventional oil fields. Similar problems on a smaller scale in the UK were found (and solved) in Lincolnshire by BP at their Gainsborough Oilfield in 1959, where the field underlies the nearby village, and at Wareham, Dorset where the oilfield underlies the town. The main problem in the UK compared to the USA, is that there are fewer or no local people with any vested interest in the success of these projects.'

According to the Guardian 'Over a few years since commercial operations began at scale, shale gas has helped consumer gas prices *in the USA* to fall by about a third; it has offered gas security to the US and Canada for maybe 100 years; compared with an estimated 18 months for the UK. In the USA it presented an opportunity to generate electricity at half the CO^2 emissions of coal.'

Re-fracturing is not a one-off process. It might have to be repeated every 4–5 years in successful wells, presumably as cracks close up. Each fracture event brings with it the possibility of further earth tremors, and potentially, pollution of the water table. Vast quantities of water are required. On average, a third of that is returned to the surface. Though it might be possible to re-use produced water by treatment or to reduce the potential environmental impact by changing the chemicals added, this has not happened; freshwater is currently needed for fracturing.

The documentary 'Gasland' showed people turning their taps on and setting light to the water. While the frackers claimed this had nothing to do with their activities, the PR damage had been done. This is despite the US industry saying they would never allow drilling at shallow depths again and so there would be no possibility of this happening in the future.

Among the backwash, the *Tyndall report* shows, are heavy metals and radioactive minerals. Fracking fluids can contaminate water supplies; either through the cracks forced open in the rocks, or through drilling too near to aquifers. In the US this seems to have happened repeatedly. The Tyndall Centre claimed that water supplies would be contaminated by methane bubbling out through the cracks.

Even if the whole world were to switch from coal to shale gas, the climate benefits of doing so through reduced CO^2 emissions could be easily offset by such fugitive methane leakages, according to the US National Centre for Atmospheric Research (NCAR). This is significant, the global warming potential (GWP) of methane is 72 times that of carbon dioxide.

Scientists have been surprised by a surge in methane, which began just over 10 years ago, in 2007, and is accelerating. It is believed that the majority is coming from melting tundra. Concentrations over just those three years (2014–2017), rose by more than 20 parts per billion, bringing the total to 1,830ppb.

Fracking had become an energy security issue. The argument goes like this 'Which is better, though, for the UK to consume oil and gas found on its doorstep or to import it at great cost, and environmental damage, from thousands of miles away, often from…dubious regimes?' Switching from coal to gas is cheap – and it cuts emissions by roughly half. It doesn't solve the climate change problem in the long run, but it gets emissions down much faster and much cheaper than all those offshore wind farms in the short to medium term.

The EU has inexplicably classed shale gas as low-carbon, allowing funds allocated for renewables to be used instead of for sun or wind. By definition, however, it is a finite resource, it cannot be renewed. The Tory government has conspired to overthrow the planning system, and steamroller through a blanket green light to exploration. According to Paul Mobbs: 'The clear way out of the climate crisis we face is to develop renewable sources of energy to build a low, ultimately zero, carbon economy as fast as possible. There is no place here for the exploitation of any new fossil fuels and especially those that carry a high intrinsic risk of a variety of damaging environmental impacts, like shale gas. This is a critical decision for the UK and for the world—*are we going to build the zero-carbon economy we need to avert climate catastrophe, as fast as possible—or will we endlessly defer that goal as we exploit every last drop of every new source of fossil fuel we can find,* until it's too late, and we are facing disasters a hundred times worse than, for instance, the one we are seeing now in Somalia?'

The duplicitous nature of Tory party energy policy, whether on fracking or the U-turn over Heathrow to the curtailing of solar subsidy, the lie about the 'green new deal' is apparent. The government stated they would not allow exploration under national parks, but promptly broke this promise by use of a statutory instrument. Not that it is clear that any oil company would want to risk the publicity of drilling there. The quick fix from policies stolen from the Greens.

A lot of people (though few of the campers) would think that only the government can ultimately tackle climate change. The IPCC had noted, however: 'Stronger efforts at the international level do not necessarily lead to substantive and rapid results at the local level (high confidence).'

Oil Tar Sands

Around Kingsnorth, activists had established an information centre in Gillingham – the *Tipping Point* coffee shop. Ironically, this shop was to wash its hands of politics nine months later – and become a Community Centre sponsored by BP. This had unexpected consequences.

'The *Tipping Point* shop has been *cleared of political content* as part of the new sponsorship deal – but the tea and coffee remain fair trade.' Bought off as part of BP's corporate responsibility program, it was intended to offset poor community relations caused by the company operations in other parts of the world.

In a breathtakingly frank admission, BP's Joanna King explained, 'We understand that our investment in environmentally destructive schemes, such as the Canadian tar sands, tends to generate a lot of bad feelings aimed at our brand. While we are not prepared to pass up such profitable opportunities, we are happy to buy biscuits for people in Medway in order to offset accusations of callous disregard to the well-being of people elsewhere.'

This might have been a red rag to a bull, because, on 14 January 2011, a group of protesters invaded the *Department of Business, Innovation and Skills* in London. They demanded a meeting with Stephen Green, the new minister for Trade. Calling themselves the *Big Society Trade Negotiators*, they believed that trade negotiations between the EU and Canada, due to start in Brussels the following

Monday, would dramatically boost Europe's involvement in the *Canadian Tar Sands* – the most destructive project on earth. These deposits, located mainly in the far north of the province of Alberta, are the world's second-largest oil reserves, but they are impure. Bitumen, a viscous tarry oil, needs lots of high-energy and chemical processing – one reason it's widely considered the world's dirtiest oil. The (environmental) cost of the current tar sands extraction in Canada is immense. Two tonnes of oil sands produce just one barrel—42 gallons—of usable crude (Chevron figures). In order to extract the bitumen from the oil sands, the ore is mixed with warm water to create a slurry. This is then fed into a processing unit, in which the bitumen is separated from the water and sand mixture. The extracted bitumen is diluted with a solvent before being sent via the XL pipeline to an upgrading facility near Edmonton (the 'Keystone' project). There, it will be transformed into a wide range of premium low-sulphur and low-viscosity synthetic crude oils. It was then to be pumped into the pipeline through the mid-west which is under construction.

Extraction produces 'tailings', a mixture of sand, water, clay, silt, hydrocarbons and toxic chemicals that are left behind after processing, as massive lake deposits, with no way of disposing of the toxic mix they hold. Some, like naphthenic acid, are carcinogenic. These lakes are large enough to be seen from space: the Environmental Defence report contains some striking images demonstrating this, as well as detailed information on toxic aquatic pollution, unexplained cancer clusters in local populations, and increasing problems of air pollution in Canada.

Permission has finally been granted for the TransCanada Keystone XL Pipeline…to construct, connect, operate and maintain pipeline facilities for the import of oil from Canada to the United States. The project had been paused in 2018, following a re-assessment of potential oil spills and other environmental impacts of the pipeline and is now on hold again. The pipeline would have taken crude oil from tar sands in western Canada right the USA from the Montana border to the Gulf Coast of the USA. It has now been postponed by the Biden administration. The metropolitan campers conducted a comprehensive teach-in about Tar Sands. George Poitras, a native of the Mikisew Cree First Nation, came to the London camp to speak. The EU and Canada have negotiated an ambitious free trade deal (CETA, the *Comprehensive Economic and Trade Agreement*) that has in 2016, opened up the European market to imports of carbon-intensive Tar Sands oil for the first time (see the previous chapter). Though the EC had included a 'reference value' for tar sands in a key piece of European law, the *Fuel Quality Directive*, this is the first time this highly polluting product has been approved over our side of the Atlantic.

According to the EU Executive, tar sand derived fuel is 23% more carbon-intensive than conventional oil. The most controversial aspect of CETA is to allow multinational companies like BP and Shell to sue national governments over social and environmental regulations they disagree with.

'In addition, exploitation has led to the displacement of indigenous people and deforestation on a mass scale: Only a small part of over 138,000 square km of boreal forest peat bog (known as muskeg) has so far been exploited,' George Poitras, told the campers that so-called tar sand extraction schemes were violating treaty rights and putting the lives of locals at risk. He said: 'We are seeing a terrifyingly high rate of cancer in Fort Chipewyan, where I live. We are convinced these cancers are linked to the tar sands development on our doorstep.' At the same time, he went on to acknowledge it had provided well-paid employment.

The industry thought it would be easier to export oil through the US heartland rather than the obvious, shorter pipe route through the Rocky Mountains to Canada's west coast, via the proposed Northern Gateway pipeline. Apparently because of opposition from native Canadians; 'The oil industry would have done the shorter Northern Gateway route first but gambled that resistance to the pipeline would be far weaker in the US mid-west,' IPS was told. However, opposition in the USA was massive, with nearly 1000 arrests. As I write, the proposed XL pipeline is unfinished.

Chapter 18

Edinburgh (August 19–25, 2010)

There was a final autumn camp that year that involved the targeting of the RBS HQ just outside Edinburgh. This was a deflated affair compared to previous camps; the shadow of the Ratcliffe arrests hung heavy on the movement.

'In place of simple poverty, we have loans and credit ratings – we are not a class without property, but a class driven by debt. And once again, all this appears voluntary, or even as "progress". It was something I could identify with, as I had sold my flat at a considerable loss following the banking collapse.'

The RBS HQ employed some 3000 staff in Edinburgh. Climate Camp claimed that RBS, which was an 84% government-owned bank, had lent out a quarter of the cash given by the government bailout to coal, oil and gas companies for exploration. Ian Fraser, (an award-winning journalist with the Financial Times) noted: '...of the $15 billion of funding provided by RBS to the energy sector since its October 2008 bailout, only $83m, (a twentieth), went to alternative energy.' *People and Planet,* the student organisation, called on RBS to calculate and publish the embedded emissions resulting from loans to oil, gas and coal companies and projects, cap embedded emissions and set annual targets for reductions and commit to a complete transition from fossil fuel to renewable energy lending Establish 'no-go' areas for lending: immediately halt loans to unconventional fossil fuels (such as tar sands) and which affect sensitive ecosystems such as rain forests. They called for funding for new unabated coal power generation in the global North to be stopped.

The campers ridiculed a tokenistic section of the RBS website dealing with carbon offsetting, which suggested recycling and switching off unwanted lights. This, they maintained, was somewhat farcical when it was investing so heavily in carbon-intensive fossil fuel development. Edinburgh-based oil company *Cairn Energy* had borrowed £100 million from RBS to start drilling in the so-called 'Iceberg Alley' (an area of the Davis Straits off the coast of Greenland). This was close to where the Petermann glacier recently broke away. It was on the basis of this loan that Cairn was able to move forward the drilling by one year. In the event, the sell struck dry. The activists would use a pig filled with molasses in a street demonstration.

The *Daily Telegraph*, among others, was unsympathetic:

'In their arrogant desire to justify anything and everything connected with *this sort of protest*, these unashamed apologists for illegality ignore the fact that it is taxpayer-funded policemen who are caught in the middle, trying on the one hand to allow peaceful demonstrations but vilified if they act against law-breakers.'

'You actively encourage protesters to take actions as far as they see fit, and provide legal information to help them do so. You count on impressionable folk to listen to your encouragement to do things like this and for that reason, you are just as guilty. Here, this is what actually happened, not like that PR bull you send out making it look like you are all peaceful earth-loving people.'

According to the CCA website, a mere 100 activists had set up camp at around 9.15 pm on Wednesday, 19 August, a day earlier than expected – in the usual pre-emptive swoop. This was apparently a completely different (and smaller) set of campers from previous years. It ran on to 25 August. It was not one sold on NVDA, either.

There was, surprisingly, no attempt by RBS to deny the space. 'The land that RBS essentially conceded was a lush grassy strip along the valley stream…split naturally into 2 sections, one overlooking the offices, and the other nicely surrounded by trees, and all portioned from RBS large and boringly smart building with impeccably mown lawns by a creek with a couple of bridges spanning it.' Regarding the camp, an RBS spokesperson stated: 'The impact of this on our customers and operations is negligible to nil.'

The Lothian and Borders Police mounted 'Operation Octave' to protect the RBS HQ. The weeklong demonstration and spin-off protests cost £649,600. This was actually the cheapest police operation in relation to any camp; the average was millions.

There was property damage; the breaking of windows was condemned, not just by 'pacifist' campers, but by two of the invited speakers – indigenous Canadians from the oil tar sand zone (see Chapter 20). They described themselves as 'guests' of the Climate Camp and as representing their nation,

219

the 'Frog Clan'. Back in Canada, they were responsible for their activities abroad, they say, and feel they can no longer stay at the camp. They ask for 'respect' from the campers and that their workshop (which was interrupted by the incursion towards RBS) was rescheduled. The camp seemed to be split, or unsure how to react. While some had strongly defended 'property destruction' as part of a 'diversity of tactics', others apologise unreservedly for it. Only one person even commented that we should 'not put indigenous peoples on a pedestal'. It was not a misstep.

As was *the Lady*. The magazine wrote: 'Damaging property has become a tactic that many activists feel is acceptable, as long as people aren't injured. Is this the point at which the principles of nonviolence start to fray? *What would we do in the context of a society where the strong violently protect their own interests against the justifiable demands of the weak?'* (Author's emphasis) It might be very productive to organise viewings of 'Nonviolence for a Change' and debate that particular moral dilemma in the light of current affairs: the Arab Spring, the death of Ian Tomlinson, undercover police infiltrating protest groups'. These issues continue with the *Extinction Rebellion.*

The molassapult – a giant ballista-style catapult, was the new siege weapon set to be deployed at this camp, but there was to be no civil war re-enactment. Truly, it was *Edinburgh fringe* material. Previewed on the net as '...great for smearing oil-like substances high up on the walls of corporate bad guys'. The rhino's deployment turned out to be more farce than action. Built on wheels some distance away from the RBS, it took some 50 activists, 'armed' with bows and arrows, with painted faces and animal masks, more than 3 hours to pull and push it in front of the police lines.

A marquee that stood in its way had to be swiftly taken down, just like a few branches of a tree (after much discussion and apology to the tree) that marked the rhino's slow progress towards RBS HQ. It was never used. It ended with a collision with the bonnet of a police van, amidst shaking of heads and murmurs of the 'Camp for Climate Comedy'. The police had decided to erect a metal fence at the main gate, which simply stopped the Rhino in its tracks. This incident ended with a standoff which continued until the end of camp.

The deteriorating consensus-building process meant that one group of people—trying to hold the line, trying to protect a site with a human blockade—was persuaded to give up their position by those who weren't themselves holding the line. 'I think this shows a lack of a culture of solidarity, as well as of a culture of consensus. Thankfully, this year (unlike Bishopsgate the previous) this did not lead to a violent and traumatising rout, merely to a loss of strategic advantage.'

Climate Camp had its own Twitter feed, of course, but anyone browsing through the '#climatecamp' hashtag would probably not have got the impression of the day's events that the spinsters at Climate Camp intended. Supportive texts were swamped by 'fake' tweeters ridiculing the activists or even pretending to be them.

The Climate Camp media office spelt out its frustration in a press release:

'The greater the current economic downturn, the less we hear about climate change or other so-called environmental and 'green' concerns; it was ever thus, which is why this lot has to resort to a high-profile attack that's concentrated in the main against an outfit like RBS, which is not the UK's most popular concern at the moment.'

At the same time, affinity groups were active. Over twenty different autonomous actions took place across Scotland, with open cast coalmines being shut down, the headquarters of oil and mining companies being occupied, as well as several branches of RBS. The Port of Leith, RBS Drummond House and even the Edinburgh Fringe were among the targets. The Clydesdale Bank in Lothian Road was spray-painted; while campaigners took over the RBS sponsored stage at the Edinburgh fringe to perform a dance routine to an alternative version of Lady Gaga's then number one smash hit *Poker Face*.

Property damage had won no friends. This was to be the last breath of this brand. Many campers would go on to attend the Copenhagen meeting of the COP. Meanwhile, the planet is heating up. Hot weather is being caused by the strong global heating trend being driven by carbon emissions and local variability. Extreme temperatures were estimated to have led to 3400 deaths between 2016-2019 in the UK.

Chapter 19

Others Move in to the Vacuum

By 2011, the schisms between reformists and radicals, together with the core consensus decision-making process, became undeniable.

Even class issues had reared their ugly head. As *SchNews* blog put it: 'they came, they camped, they conquered (well, not quite). During a soul-searching Dorset retreat, Climate Camp has decided to suspend tent-centred activism – citing the "radically different political landscape" of 2011.'

This paragraph stands out:

'Having been through Drax, Kingsnorth, Heathrow, RBS, Copenhagen and one helluva lot of hummus, the group are now turning their attention to coordination with the wider anti-cuts and anti-austerity movement.' In what seems to be a direct attack on the autonomous, grass-roots affinity groups, a small number of the 'old guard' came to the national planning meeting on 21–26 February with their own agenda to kill Climate Camp, *despite a block and four stand-asides in the 'consensus' process'*.

On the first day the proposal to dissolve the shared national identity of Climate Camp had reached an impasse with six blocks to the decision, members in favour of dissolution fought back with what has now been termed as the 'anti-block' – the threat to leave the group if the decision didn't pass. *Despite the normal conventions of consensus decision-making*, and the statement published on the website following the meeting, the proposal was carried forward without consensus, ignoring the Delphi process. As the financial crisis unfolded, we moved to directly target the root cause of airport expansion and coal-fired power stations: our economic system…in October 1,000 people were poised to shut down Ratcliffe-on-Soar power station, in Nottinghamshire, a major carbon emitter owned by E.On the energy giant behind the Kingsnorth plans. In December, many travelled on Climate Camp coaches to Copenhagen as part of our affiliation to the international direct action network Climate Justice Action, against the skewed UN negotiations known as COP 15. *Despite much success, weaknesses in our organisational structures and processes were exposed within our networks.* Meanwhile, later that same month, affinity action continued. Members of *Rising Tide* were blockading the Coryton oil distribution centre. By 2009, enthusiasm for organising environment events was on the wane; partly following the failure of Copenhagen, not in my opinion just because of police action, per se. The fracture of cohesion, the lack of direction and the nuclear split; unresolved issues, and the police encroachment (see later chapter).

The official version released in February 2011 on the website was somewhat incoherent: 'The near-collapse of the financial system; droughts in the Amazon, floods in Pakistan; a new government in the UK; a violent program of unprecedented cuts; food prices rising and real incomes eroding; revolutions across the Middle East…This is all very different from 2005 when the Camp for Climate Action first met to spark radical action on the greatest threat to humanity, climate change.'

The core belief in Non-Violent Direct Action was being questioned, possibly by people who had never accepted it. In America, it was being tarred as Marxism. 'Agenda 21', to many Americans, it seemed, was another attack on their God-given individualism. There was a bad feeling about group dynamics among campers as well. This consensus decision-making blog is typical:

'(Consensus)…militates against scientifically thrashing out ideas, or any real notion of commitment to common struggle or accountability—no one is obliged to do anything they don't want to do.'

As the earlier quote: '…you actively encourage protesters to take actions as far as they see fit, and provide legal information to help them do so. You count on impressionable folk to listen to your encouragement to do things like this and for that reason, you are just as guilty.'

Unable to agree with a policy direction, one fruitless meeting led to another. One frustrated blogger wrote, 'I think Climate Camp could seriously benefit from providing answers to a lot of questions that it is increasingly presented with, like:

- Does Climate Camp support a diversity of direct action tactics? If so, how does it support them?
- What is the aim of mass action and media spectacle?
- What is the long – term strategy?

- Does consensus decision making actually work on a mass scale with hundreds of people?
- How does this hub function in regard to regional groups?
- How much say does each have in decisions?
- Does consensus decision making, in fact, work in all situations...?

Nevertheless, the main effect is that as people join the process, they are not being informed about the underlying politics, and in this vacuum, they place their own preconceptions.

- What is the Climate Camp "policy" in regard to decentralisation of the 'organisation' and regional autonomy? Need to train others up before handing over.'

'...It is apparent that there is a need for two things. Firstly, greater visibility for the anarchist roots within the day-to-day life of the CCA process and proposals. Secondly, and just as importantly, a more open and explicit critique of capitalism and how it is the root cause of climate change.'

Both Drax and Heathrow were fairly radical camps offering solutions to climate change, using alternative ideas to those proposed in the mainstream. However, the call for direct action was a poor bedfellow to the call for more state intervention, requiring a higher degree of obedience. Memorably, George Monbiot apologised to 'the anarchists in the crowd for his belief in state intervention,' adding 'This issue is compounded by the inevitable tendency of more militant campaigners being drawn to the barricades and defending the camp against police'.

On the other hand: 'It is a symptom of wider systemic oppression, which cannot be tackled without addressing these underlying causes and argue against the short-term, state-led, being promoted by a minority. So why are people pissed off with the direction the camp has taken? Should we not just be happy with the huge amount of people who have attended the four camps and the equally huge amount of publicity we have attracted around environmental issues regardless of how we got it?'

But these blogs were just the start. The mainstream media was also tired of this annual spectacle. *Its obsession with structure, its relationship with media and police* were cited in 2009 by Peter Beaumont in his *Observer* column, as a major hindrance to outreach. He believed it lacked *...a series of achievable goals that those outside the camp movement could easily identify with. The majority of people come to anti-capitalist conclusions through a process of struggle rooted in their everyday life.* Beaumont also believed they should have singled out individual figures to act as the *'personification...of a particular evil...'* rather than abstract ideas. As they were ideologically opposed to leadership *per se*, this was never likely to happen. He believed some level of concern about losing credibility was to be expected.

These remarks, he believed, could also be applicable to significant sectors of the wider anti-war and anti-globalisation movement. 'They have struggled either to articulate precisely what their message is (other than negative). We want to take strong positions that can be backed up by solid research and sound science, and we want to communicate those to the public and the media in the most persuasive way possible,' he continued. The fear of ridicule is based on a major false assumption as well, that the media are just waiting to tell the public and say, 'Aha! We told you they were crazy!'

While new recruits were still coming along, for Lauren Wroe, co-founder of critical blog '*Shift*', the experience of Heathrow brought concerns as much as inspiration. 'All the ideas about austerity, forcibly limiting people's lifestyles and restricting their movement – it didn't fit with a radical politics of climate change,' she wrote. The camp's direct action, Lauren felt, was also becoming problematic. 'It was being used more as a government lobby tool. The urgency of the situation was making people turn toward the state for solutions, and *put aside questions of social change* – it was effectiveness first, equity second.'

What followed was a long period of talking, (not dissimilar to Brexit), AND as little to show for it. These were all about points of doctrine. A July 2010 blog on the website illustrates this:

'Any National Climate Change Coalition should exist to:-

Raise awareness about the gravity and urgency of the threat from climate change and second, to pressure those with the greatest power to take effective action to do so with the utmost speed and resolution;

Recognise that supporters will have different and *deeply held* differences in ways of preventing climate change and that open debate and understanding is necessary to strengthen the movement; demonstrate the enormous potential power of a united social movement.'

At this time, Regional actions were to replace the annual camp, so that the *Camp for Climate Action* could be an all-year-round network. The aim, according to their website, was to give neighbourhoods more space so they had longer gaps between the UK gatherings. The neighbourhood structure was not a well-adapted vehicle to such a change. Only the Midlands barrio went on to do something.

Blogger Giulio Sica complained, 'The environmental movement has been taken over by technocrats – marketing men and capitalists in green disguise. Until the debt-based financial system is replaced with one that reflects the reality of our finite resources, all the talk of CO^2 will change nothing. We need to get the majority back on the side of ecology and that will not happen while we focus on computer models and scientific jargon at the expense of the existential concerns of habitat conservation, recycling and local clean energy generation.' Naomi Klein has also drawn attention to elitism in the environmental movement, something the Campers had studiously attempted to avoid.

A similar situation to what happened at Copenhagen in 2009!

Veteran camp campaigners then attempted to re-formulate their debate on radical climate throughout 2011, initially at *Space for Change* in January at Monkton Wyld Court in Dorset, then *Common Ground* meeting in June, At this workshop in June 2011, nostalgia for an annual event continued, despite its cancellation that February. This was symptomatic of the indecision that set in. Edinburgh would be the last; facilitators admitted the workshop hasn't managed to build a coherent and united community, which effective consensus should. (Website) The 'what next' exercises *continued* with a splinter group forming the *Climate Justice Collective.* CJC's approach to activism was networking with others. Finally, two 'New Directions' meetings were held in July: '…this meeting is for people who have previously been involved in organising the Camp for Climate Action, or other radical grassroots climate action, and feel positive about working together.' The facilitators' group formed at 'New Directions Part 1' was expected to arrange 'New Directions 2'.

Critics waded in: 'The *Metamorphosis* Statement published after this blatant disregard for due process, reads like a bizarre non-linear mix of self-congratulation and random keywords. Citing events like "…droughts in the Amazon, floods in Pakistan; food prices rising (and) revolutions across the Middle East" which have created a world "very different from 2005 when the *Camp for Climate Action* first met" it emphasises a need to change. Boxing Day tsunami, Hurricane Katrina, oil price rises due to trouble in the Middle East, occupation of Iraq? All around 2005. And aren't extreme weather conditions that cause floods and droughts essentially climate change issues?' *A statement that apparently was not agreed collectively, but written afterwards – by one of those who had proposed the disbanding of the network.*

The government took the 'you're either with us or against us' rhetoric of the War on Terrorism, a black and white mentality, and applied it to activists of any hue. Fighting the system's agents is less important than breaking down the self-alienation which underpins it. If activists don't prove they are 'with us' by condemning sabotage, then they are clearly 'against us' and one with the 'terrorists'. One blogger put it this way: 'Perhaps the intellectual surrender is so complete because the forces we hoped would make the world a more civilised place of freedom—personal freedom, democracy, material advance, technological power—are in truth paving the way to its destruction. The powers we most trusted have betrayed us, which we believed would save us now threatens to devour us.'

Typically many of those originally involved (including myself) had long before drifted away to do other things. 'For Tamsin, age 25, founder of *Climate Rush*, this realisation that the future of the green movement lies in it becoming as diverse as possible crystallised in Copenhagen...amid a moment of panic when she feared she had been disowned. She had prompted a spat from some activists in *Plane Stupid* (the climate change group she had originally joined) who said she would no longer be welcomed or invited to events.'

Climate Rush was a movement modelled on the *Suffragettes*, attempting to mobilise feminists for mass actions, even down to adopting their branding – diagonal red sashes. Their website promoted practical contributions to the process of mitigation and adaptation to climate change; insulating lofts or helping with climate disaster relief.

'I find this difficult...but the reality is that the mainstream has embraced the green movement and it's important for us to grow up and embrace the mainstream.' She went on to join the 'Save our Forests' campaign when the Forestry Commission was up for privatisation.

This ignores what was learned by doing, the skills learned that were transferable – the use of flash mobs. *UK Uncut* and the *Extinction Rebellion*, for example. Other issues: Poverty, the financial crisis and racism were getting worse, so climate change has fallen off the radar. 647 000 under-eighteens found their Educational Maintenance Allowances withdrawn.

Writing in the *Guardian* in the summer of 2011, Susanna Rustin argued:

'This feeling of a missed opportunity. And of 2009, as a high-water mark in public engagement with the (green) issues finds many echoes. Though activists trumpet their recent success in having seen off a third runway at Heathrow, and a new fleet of coal-fired power stations, as well as helping the UK to commit the UK to a strict timetable for cutting emissions, they admit that the disappointment after Copenhagen, and uncertainty about the future, have been difficult to manage.'

By 27 October 2010, *UK Uncut* only existed as *#ukuncut*, a Twitter hashtag someone had invented the night before the Vodafone protest. The high-profile flash mobbing of companies accused of using tax havens to short-change the British Exchequer attracted support and publicity. The speed of which took the police off guard for once.

#ukuncut began trending around the UK and people began to talk about replication. Protest methods once known to a committed few were adopted by the uncommitted mass, wrote Paul Mason. The idea went viral. Seething anger about the cuts had found an outlet. Just three days later, close to thirty Vodafone stores had been occupied around the country.

By November, social media, particularly Twitter and blackberry, was in widespread use organising UK protests. 'On 24 November school walkouts began in cities and towns all-round the UK'. This was in part owing to the withdrawal of the *Educational Maintenance Allowance*, a means-tested subsidy for 16 to 19-year-olds to persuade them to stay in education after 'O' levels. This had been of substantial benefit to less fortunate pupils.

On 26 February 2011, *UkUncut* had organised the 'Big Society Bail-in', targeting around 100 Lloyds TSB, NatWest and RBS branches up and down the country. The logic of this occupation tactic (was) beautiful in its simplicity: all across the board, the government was implementing a series of stringent and ideologically motivated austerity measures as it picked up the tab from the financial crash. The banks, however, were deemed too big to fail and, unlike the public, had the ear (and support) of the government. If there is one place where public services can ride out the storm—be they laundry services, childcare facilities or libraries—it is in a bank.

Like Climate Camp, *UkUncut* also ran into skirmishes with the police. This came to a head in March 2011, when 145 of them were arrested after being kettled at Fortnum and Mason. The 'black bloc', some 400 strong, were not. Does that mean they were less of a threat than UkUncut?

The disbanding of the *Camp for Climate Action movement* was, perhaps surprisingly, welcomed by several PR organisations as a positive sign for environmental activism. Forster director Peter Gilheany welcomed the move. 'Climate Camps were great *as part of their time* because they raised awareness very quickly,' he said. 'But since it is becoming *such a political issue*, what we now need are mainstream messages around climate change. It is not just about climate change – it is about justice, transport, public health, and so on. It is all about being issue-specific.'

Futerra co-founder, Solitaire Townsend, saw the disbanding as a sign that climate protest was moving away from an 'angry and anti' standpoint to 'angry and inspired'. She said: 'The *10:10 campaign* is the best example of this in the UK. (This was the crowd-funded Fanny Adams film, *Age of Stupid*). It continues to bring together campaigners, businesses and even government in *solutions-focused* campaigning, rather than shouting about the problems.' This was a limited screening, but Hollywood responded to this film with a few fantastical sci-fi blockbusters, films like *Avatar, Blade Runner,* and *Inception.*

In May 2012, 300 protesters belonging to the *Climate Justice Coalition* attempted to disrupt an energy summit in the City of London, in an event supported by groups including *UkUncut, Fuel Poverty Action and the Campaign against Climate Change.* This was the first active sign of progress in two years.

A blogger wrote: 'Well done Climate Campers for all the popular education, activist training, political consciousness-raising, dedication and commitment. Through your efforts, a new generation of activists are tooled up and buoyed with the experience and confidence needed to keep going with all the social and environmental justice work going on…'

David King (government adviser) argued that the UK's 2008 Climate Change Act—at that time the most ambitious legally binding emissions target in the world—along with actions such as its early engagement with China on global warming, should have put the UK at the forefront of global negotiations on climate action in the run-up to the UN summit in Copenhagen in 2009. (It is only now in 2020 that China has pledged to reach zero emissions by 2060). This summit, attended by scores of world leaders, was a great disappointment once again. Only 100 world leaders were ready to take incremental measures.

The Danish police seemed ready to brutalise any observers. Durban 2011 was the follow-up. New extraction opportunities like 'fracking', and issues such as 'zero waste' had arrived on the scene, muddying the consensus.

Trade unions were finally getting on board. Two road shows toured England in spring 2012. The climate issue would not go away: '…we learned that 2010 carbon emissions had reached roughly 1,000 tonnes per second after the world's miraculous "economic recovery".'

The EU Commission vowed to block the relocation of companies in other regions not complying with similar legislation—by granting some free allocations of CO^2 emissions provided that they were at least at the same level as a benchmark. (About one-third)

There followed a few years where very little happened. Then came Greta…

Moving forward to 2018, the *UK student climate network* movement and other international student groups had been out in force. *Rising Up*/the *Extinction Rebellion* has the following aims:

- To support and encourage a citizens uprising in the UK (of about 2 million people) involving low level and higher risk acts of civil disobedience by some (with others willing to support those that take actions).
- When ready, create a participatory, democratic process that discusses and improves a draft manifesto

for change and a new constitution. This will involve creating a genuine democracy, alongside an economy to maximise well-being and minimise harm. (According to the UkUncut website).

'In April 2019, the *Extinction Rebellion* forced London to a standstill in a ten-day protest, with more than 1,100 people arrested. More than a million pupils participated in a Greta-inspired school strike in March, and many have continued to strike weekly as part of the *#FridaysForFuture movement.*' In 2020, the group had to call off their spring protest; the coronavirus crisis already showing what a world with less pollution would look like. It has then resumed activity in September blockading newspaper-printing works, with 80 arrests.

The slogan 'listen to the science', popularised by the *Extinction Rebellion,* imagines change as a process of pressuring politicians to improve existing economic, social and political systems. There are experts working out the details for a proposed bill: 'Climate and Ecological Emergency Bill'. This called for the *Climate Assembly UK,* to be created from the grassroots. The bill would incorporate 'the common but differentiated responsibilities and respective capabilities' of the Paris accord.

In many ways, then, XR mirrors the affinity group model the campers used. A flexible, decentralised supportive structure was duplicated. For example, semi-naked climate change protesters interrupted a Commons debate on Brexit as they stripped off their clothes in the public gallery. Several *'Extinction Rebellion'* embers had glued themselves to the dividing window of MPs from the watching public, in the worst Commons security breach since 2014. Labour MP Peter Kyle joked about the 'naked truth' as MPs' were distracted from his speech in April 2020.

Climate Assembly UK reported in September 2020; designed so that our MP Representatives might be willing to make the first move. The assembly had a strong preference for information and education to help the public make informed choices. They were also adamant that greener products and services should be affordable and accessible to all.

Members were willing to countenance reducing car use by up to 5% each decade and lowering meat and dairy consumption by 20%-40% by 2050. They seemed reluctant to propose extensive legal restrictions but did support a rapid ban on the sale of the most polluting vehicles. They also favoured legislating a faster move to electric vehicles than current government plans.

Meanwhile, the extent of the changes that human actions are wreaking on the planet are accelerating. Last week, a separate team of scientists found that melting of the Antarctic ice cap would continue even if the world met the Paris agreement goal of holding temperature rises to no more than 2C, and would eventually raise sea levels by 2.5 metres at that level of heating.

Chapter 20

The Failure of Horizontality and 'Domestic Extremism'

'The land squats have always been the most effective and interesting thing about Climate Camp, particularly at Heathrow, where the single gesture of residing on a piece of land adjacent to the proposed runway, strip-mined an otherwise buried network of ownership and speculation. The other actions that extend out from the camp rarely achieve such revelatory eloquence.' At Heathrow, this included marking out the position of the proposed runway – with international media in attendance.

'An Awkward Position: It seems well-understood that Climate Camp is a strange meeting point for many types of activists: fluffy and spiky, anarchist and socialist, those who believe in media spectacle and those who believe in direct action, localists and globalists, geeks, freaks and lovers. *A culture of consensus is not, however, a culture of compromise*: it means we respect each other's individuality and autonomy while finding ways we can work together. So I don't believe that Climate Camp can synthesise all these different aims and intentions. That's why our support for a diversity of tactics is essential.'

'We use a diversity of tactics not just to struggle against oppression and destruction and this insane culture on every front at once, trying desperately to find something that works, though we do that; we use a diversity of tactics and respect and show solidarity with others' tactics because that's what it means to work in a mutually empowering way.'

To those looking in from the outside, like the *Daily Mail,* it seemed that 'The eco-freaks created their very own gulags and voluntarily turned themselves into the inmates. There could be no better advertising of the kind of world in which they want us all to live'. Entering protest camps, protesters were often searched by the police; then, on the other side, they would be welcomed by the volunteers within the camp. This border crossing experience created a tangible sense of entering a new space.

'When people come to Climate Camp, the biggest thing they realise is that it's full of ordinary people, with ordinary jobs who are not against the political system at all. Just frustrated by it,' said Jess Gold, Friends of the Earth campaigner and camp protester.

Former *Campaign against Climate Change* national coordinator Phil Thornhill was among those who had felt uncomfortable about the anarchist wing of the Camp model. He noted that while it had benefited from the support of respected individuals (citing MP Norman Baker), that its anarchist minority could lose its wider sympathy. The *Extinction Rebellion* is tarred with the same brush.

'It is not so much that it is illegal but that at the heart of an anarchy-based philosophy is one that doesn't admit the relevance of government.'

The majority of people come to anti-capitalist conclusions through a process of struggle rooted in their everyday life. Insurrection differs from a revolution in being an attack on the existence of state power, rather than a seizure of such power. It follows in the tradition of Walter Benjamin's idea of 'law-destroying violence', which is directed against the capability of using violence to make or preserve laws. When the consciousness of the latent presence...Force is misused for unjust ends of violence; the institution disappears, the institution falls into decay.

If the criterion established by positive law to assess the legality of violence can be analysed with regard to its meaning, then the sphere of its application must be criticised with regard to its value.

'Bonanno's theory of insurrection relies on a concept of *social war*, which alludes to the irreducible antagonism between included and excluded. Rejecting alienation invokes both an affirmation of life and desire and also an assault on the structures of power. Unfortunately, civil war is an obligatory road which must be passed in any historical moment of profound, radical transformation.' As 'Dragonowl' writes, '(Capitalism) has corroded all its deep supports, such as legal due process and civil rights, as too costly to maintain'. 'Insurrection pits active force against reactive force, and is the point of explosion of accumulated discontent'. This anarchy, I believe, sits uneasily with NVDA. It fits perfectly with affinity groups, though.

Mark Kennedy (aka Stone), a major organiser, was finally exposed in October 2009 after his girlfriend discovered a passport bearing his real name. His false name passport (Mark Stone) had by then been withdrawn by the police. His girlfriend had grown suspicious about his past and then she came across his original passport. Following research in Northern Ireland, it transpired that he had been a police officer ever since1994, and had a family there.

The Camp for Climate Action press office commented:

'We welcome the collapse of the police spy network *Operation Pegasus*, whose aim is to infiltrate extreme left-wing groups in the United Kingdom, that for years has been targeting our movement and demand they stay out. These extraordinary revelations pose a number of profound questions that now need to be answered. So far the only inquiry that's been announced will see the police investigating themselves, which is unacceptable given the indisputable evidence that officers have misled MPs and the public about the nature of their spying operation.' (One of the inquiries was delayed so that one officer could retire early to avoid censure).

'Mark was extremely good at making people trust him, his personality was perfect for getting tongues wagging. This striving to rise higher in the world of activist credentials is damaging and divisive. Most activism that goes on in the UK is not rocket science. We shouldn't be chasing after some illusive mystique of the "bigger boys".' Using his fake passport, "Mark Stone" aka Kennedy had, in six years, visited more than 22 countries, took part in protests against the building of a dam in Iceland, and toured Spain, Germany and Italy. This was all done by gaining intelligence, apparently at taxpayer expense.

'The first step must be that (Sir) Paul Stephenson and Commander Bob Broadhurst stop stonewalling and give some answers for the conduct of operations they oversaw. And they must be straight with us, not like parliament, to whom they asserted that *there were no agents in the climate movement.* In the longer term, we need to ensure that the police are no longer taking political decisions to spend millions of pounds *undermining a legitimate social movement taking action against the threat that climate change poses to us all.'* (Author's emphasis)

Private investigators had also been busy; but less consistent. One firm, *Vericola Ltd,* accidentally emailed the activists it was spying on. Corporate clients included *E.On, Scottish Power and Scottish Coal.* They had been targeting groups, including the *Camp for Climate Action and London Rising Tide* with low-level infiltration. Unlike the police, they were soon found out. Other groups were encouraged to check their lists and share any experiences. Email addresses linked to the company had been used to sign up to email lists, and *Vericola* has been employing people to attend meetings, events and actions to collect information.

Company no. 2: associated with monitoring protest groups, was *Global Open. This was* founded a decade previously by Rod Leeming, an ex-special branch officer who once ran the Animal Rights National Index. It had at least 90 clients.

Company no. 3: *Exclusive Analysis.* Revealed by photographer Marc Vallée who related how, in 2012, he had also been approached for information on protest groups.

Their particular interest was in *No Tar Sands, Rising Tide UK, Climate Camp* and *UkUncut.*

In 2018, Kennedy's girlfriend finally received documents from the police admitting that Kennedy's line manager and other officers were aware of the sexual relationship, stating 'sexual relationship with (Kate Wilson) was carried out with the acquiescence of his cover officers and line manager.' The *Undercover Research group* had this to say: 'Be aware that people who were very close to the officer may find it hard to accept the deception, and can take a long time to feel any anger towards the person they were deceived by. The manipulation of their emotions has been very complex.'

Back in January 2011, he was to sell an exclusive tale to the *Mail on Sunday*, in which he tellingly claimed four undercover officers remain in the movement. This cannot be verified. Brian Hill went on to direct *Undercover Cop*, the documentary of Mark Kennedy. This was first screened in Britain by Channel 4 on 14 November 2011. You can see it on the internet. 'Part of the film followed Kennedy during the tough period after his exposure, but Hill didn't limit himself to this traditional approach. Instead, the director sets the agent up in front of a green screen and lets him perform his own story, thereby reconstructing the key events during his work as an undercover cop…the documentary questions how far the state can go in its use of lies and deceit without losing the basic faith of its citizens.' I suppose as the Camp had refused to take part, he did not have much choice.

'Police spy Mark Kennedy infiltrated several political movements, although he is best known for his infiltration of the climate movement. After selling his story to the *Mail on Sunday*, (trying to exploit the good protester bad protester perception) it comes as no surprise that Kennedy has now cut a deal with a documentary filmmaker. No surprise either that the Camp for Climate Action media team received an email from the documentary producer, asking if we would like to be involved. Despite our usual willingness to talk to the media, we have declined the offer. Let's remember that Kennedy is a professional liar. He is so lost these days that in his most recent interview he claimed to be sad that there won't be a Climate Camp this year – and that's after systematically trying to disrupt Climate Camp activities for five years (which he clearly wasn't very good at; Heathrow and Kingsnorth still don't even have permission to be built).'

'There is absolutely nothing to gain from appearing on TV next to a habitual liar. If Kennedy wants to make himself into a national TV talking point on the psychological impacts of betrayal, that's his choice. We'll be sticking with action to tackle climate change. That's much more important than listening to Kennedy tie himself in contradictions to self-justify his seven years of deceit.'

The *Climate Collective* strongly opposed Mark Kennedy going to Denmark. Mark Kennedy was invited by the *CPH DOX* documentary film festival. He decided against appearing, claiming he was intimidated by the *Climate Collective* organisers. They wrote: 'Using undercover cops is a huge democratic problem undermining peoples' right to act politically. The fact that Mark Kennedy, and probably many of his colleagues, have been collaborating with the Danish police clearly shows how far Danish police (are) willing to go in the use of undemocratic methods in order to prevent political activism.'

'(Max) Clifford secured Kennedy an advance for this documentary (sum unknown) irrespective of the quality of its content. Having spent many years lying, and now he seems unable to know what the truth is anymore. His unreliability means that neither…police colleagues nor activist comrades wanted anything to do with the making of this film. It is a shame that a well-respected film festival has been compromised by a documentary with such a dubious basis.'

'The long-term existence of Kennedy as an undercover police officer in the movement has caused extreme emotional and psychological distress to the people who counted him as a friend, or in some cases as a partner. Some women who had sexual relations with Kennedy feel that his use of sex as a means of ingratiating himself within the community in order to obtain information was essentially state-sponsored sexual abuse. It is unacceptable for him to profit from this (film) while at the same time many people are still picking up the pieces of their lives that were shattered by his lies. You are intending to give this man a platform, and presumably, you intend to financially reward him for going over the details of how he intentionally damaged the lives of those around him. We ask you to reconsider your actions.' A group of these women has now taken the Metropolitan police to the High court and won substantial compensation three years later.

He fled to America. The police seem reluctant to re-visit his involvement. The strain of acting out of character at all times and encouraging activities which put others at risk has led to his own mental health problems and others in similar situations. *However, there is no doubt that it has been a successful tactic in defeating the so-called offence of 'domestic extremism'.*

Sir Paul Stephenson went on to forecast 'disorder on the streets' following the student riot some weeks before. This was in fact to materialise about a year later, nationwide in August 2011.

The police pursued a *divide-and-conquer* agenda – always citing the 'rogue individual' while enabling peaceful protest. This had been scaled down from the '150 hard-core protesters' claimed at Kingsnorth. The National Extremism co-ordination unit (NECTU), then affiliated to ACPO, had this to say:

'Among the people to be *targeted* are campaigners against road building and live animal exports, protesters at industrial disputes, hunt saboteurs and far-right groups. The unit will also draw up action plans that chief constables can introduce to head off the potential disorder. The move followed growing concern among police chiefs that so-called *eco-warriors* are becoming increasingly organised and creating an ever-growing threat to public order.'

The police again: 'Unfortunately, within some otherwise peaceful campaigns, *a few individuals* resort to criminal activity to further their cause. These individuals sometimes try to hide their illegal activities by associating themselves with otherwise peaceful campaigners. It is this minority which police forces, together with units like *NETCU*, are determined to stop and bring to justice.'

'Experience shows that the same people are involved in demonstrations – whether it's disruption of building works and motorways, runways, live animals for export, or people 'reclaiming' the streets. It tends to be the same people who support them and travel around the country. It's about keeping a database on them – identifying the *main* individuals.' (Assistant Commissioner Anthony Speed). Yet at Kingsnorth, they alleged there were as many as 150 hard-core troublemakers!

Essentially, every person who now attends a protest in the UK continues to be documented, catalogued and treated as someone who has, or will break the law. All because of a top-heavy conglomerate of police units, which exist simply to exist. *NETCU* define 'domestic extremism', an offence that *does not exist* in case law. The police now seem to have become a moral guardian, something Coronavirus has accelerated.

'The government also needs to give people the right to have a voice even when it is used to criticise them and let's put an end to these illegal and costly wars. I won't hold my breath on any of this happening as both the mainstream media and those paid to represent us are determined to blame anybody but themselves for the mess we have found ourselves in.'

'The broad spectrum of peaceful protest activities are a reality and presents a challenge that needs to be better reflected in the ACPO guidance.' The guidance was perceived as too vague. 'Clearly (ACPO) was created as a private company to avoid transparency, and allowed to sell the data (that we paid for) from the police National computer at such an enormous profit because it provides them with what is essentially a lucrative, hidden and unaccountable source of income, they are equally clearly using their resources against social 'crimes' and for further revenue generation. 'It was replaced by NETCU.

The *NETCU* created a handbook, *Beyond Lawful Protest: Protecting Against Domestic Extremism.* In its 2009 re-issue it states:

'The majority of protest activity in the UK is both lawful and peaceful and is carried out by law-abiding citizens who wish to exercise their freedom to assemble and protect themselves; these freedoms are an important part of our democracy and are protected within the *Human Rights Act 1998.* Unfortunately, there are a small number of people who are prepared to break the law in the belief that it will further their "cause". It is this unlawful activity, which is beyond lawful protest that we refer to as *domestic extremism.* In 2012, Police Liaison Officers were introduced to "engage" with protesters. An interesting development on the "bad cop, good cop" approach. They will have their work cut out. It falls to the Metropolitan police as the lead force who has now taken over from NECTU.'

Walter Benjamin understood this a hundred years ago: 'Rather, the "law" of the police really marks the point at which the state, whether from impotence or because of the immanent connections within any legal system, can no longer guarantee through the legal system the empirical ends that it desires at any price to attain. Therefore, the police intervene "for security reasons" in countless cases where no clear legal situation exists, when they are not merely, without the slightest relation to legal ends, accompanying the citizen as a brutal encumbrance through a life regulated by ordinances, or simply supervising him.' Whether the Mitting enquiry will be made, is another matter.

In South Wales, facial recognition is being introduced by police in Cardiff, another infringement on civil liberty, and possibly the Data Protection Act.

Keith Vaz, the chairman of the Commons home affairs select committee, had complained to the Met commissioner, Sir Paul Stephenson, and Bob Broadhurst, another commander, which they had failed to disclose 'the full facts'. 'During our inquiry into the G20 protests, (MPs) explicitly asked them about the deployment of undercover officers, I am disappointed they appear not to have given us the full facts.' At the NUJ photography conference, Sir Paul Stephenson had stated that he would listen to complaints about bigger events and more volatile strategies. This had not impressed the professional cameramen, who felt victimised.

In its approach, the *Mitting inquiry* has been accused of prioritising police over victims, keeping victims at arm's length. It would be of benefit if an approach of cooperation rather than hostility towards civilian NGOs was taken.

Another blogger wrote:

'…You try to encompass everything under the global warming banner. I find it extremely unhelpful, and (it) leads to you turning off the public who will have to pay for anything and everything in the cause of fighting "climate change". This is of course already being implemented through electricity bills rising to pay for a low-carbon generation.'

The direct action flash mobs…have hit the news. A flash mob (or flash mob) is a group of people who assemble suddenly in a public place, perform an unusual and sometimes seemingly pointless act for a brief time, then disperse, often for the purposes of entertainment, satire, artistic expression and are organised via telecoms, social media, or viral emails. They have been particularly effective for UkUncut. 'Any event that poses a constant threat of "unknown unknowns" the system cannot handle.'

Others were more optimistic: '…the ways that people work together best are based on models drawn from the carefully studied ecosystems around us and our own physical make-up. It's natural, and it's efficient. Each person has a task that's unique to them, that is their personal interest and is the focus of their own individual attention. This is how we get democracy done. By behaving like a self-organising, self-correcting ecosystem. And this is how both Social Change and Climate Change can be addressed – by small, local groups doing action, education, training and political engagement at the grassroots level…' This was also the 'Intergovernmental Panel on climate change' view: 'Stronger efforts at the international level do not necessarily lead to substantive and rapid results at the local level.'

Chapter 21
The Spin-Off Legacy

The camps, as we have seen, were a novel though not an original solution to an impasse in the story of protest. It raised serious issues for the government; it arguably influenced environmental policy. As Paul Mason put it, '...protest methods once known to a committed few were adopted by the uncommitted mass.' I am very pleased in this age of cynicism that schoolchildren worldwide are standing up to corporate power and government inaction, by forming *Student Climate Networks*. I do have reservations about the *Extinction Rebellion* because they have so far failed to provide an alternative modeller to influence government policy. As *Workers' Liberty* writes: 'However, at a certain point people will start to ask the same questions – how does sitting on a road or clogging up the courts help halt climate change? If the goal is simply "consciousness-raising" then what next? It is important that this movement does not end up in the same direct action cul-de-sac as the movements that went before it. Direct action favours those who have nothing else to offer but their own physical actions...to take a stand and risk arrest, was easier for those who had the least to lose by doing so.' Various members have been fined a total of

£200 000 for breach of Coronavirus rules, which they have been unwilling to adhere to.

Before that, Climate Camp had tried to create a process capable of bringing together hundreds of activists spread across the whole country to plan and carry out very complex action camps as well as many other activities. As one blogger wrote: 'Since its inception, Climate Camp was an amazing experiment in working by consensus, a kind of petri dish or hothouse. The process has had to be capable of dealing with large group consensus, and a structure that has included spokes-councils, emergency spokes-councils, working groups, a neighbourhood system, and open meetings. The process referred to was the *Delphi method* of NVDA.

Organisational and media skills, both to communicate externally and internally, could not be faulted. The open and democratic structure targeted property and process rather than people.

However, continually forced to seek personal and collective validation through the use of spectacle, the campers were unable to connect with the wider audience in the way the *Extinction Rebellion* has since. When even the broadsheet media started to lose sympathy with a repetitive strategy, it collapsed in short order. The tabloids led the way. They merely continued to ridicule the whole thing, as they had done all along.

Now climate protest has, once again, become much more in the public eye. The *Extinction Rebellion* and the Student climate networks are springing up, there is hope again that government policy will be updated.

In the final analysis, the Climate Camp could not continue for any number of reasons.

- The subversion of the brand; Its inability to roll out an agenda relevant to a wider audience; Its infiltration by undercover police;
- A need to move beyond preaching to the converted and start a dialogue about climate change with traditionally disengaged working audiences.

The first three of these camps (Drax, Heathrow and Kingsnorth) did contribute directly to UK legislation; the Climate Bill became law shortly after. This was a world-first achievement; it committed Britain to achieve a dramatic fall in its CO^2 outputs—a road map of targets culminating in a 60% cut by 2050—together with the cancellation of non-carbon capture coal-burning power plants. The targets set in this bill are already becoming difficult to reach and goalposts have continued to move. So far, it appears on track.

The low budget, risk-taking DIY philosophy of the campers continued to baffle and challenge the mainstream media rhetoric. It was the strength of what Paul Mason would term *unmanaged* collective labour. The trustees of many NGOs (with the exception of Greenpeace) would never have entertained such a high-risk strategy. Quite a few NGOs have seemed willing to trade their integrity for the opportunity to become 'insiders' and 'walk the corridors of power.' Many of them were reluctant to participate or have their logos on display. They agreed with the police that the anarchist minority *could lose its widespread support*. The camp legal team would go on to establish their own firm, *GBC*, which was active in supporting the 2010/2011 student movement. Other offshoots were *UkUncut* and *Occupy*.

It was leaving the system. '...the complexity and the rigidity not just of the apparatus of production as a whole but also of the economic units (firms, trusts, combines) of which it was composed, prevented any one individual gaining lived experience of the collaboration that could exist between the thousands of teams, sub-groups and groups specialised in tasks which were themselves subdivided. They could, at best, have abstract knowledge of such collaboration...but they could never gain lived experience of it from the actual collaboration they were each involved in, through their work, within their teams, workshops and so on.'.

Critics were also quick to point out the broader implication: 'If the demands of environmentalists were met, we wouldn't be able to travel far. Working life would be more labour-intensive: we wouldn't have labour-saving devices.' These factors, it was argued, would limit the potential for varied and intellectual employment, reducing opportunities for cultural experiences. Horizons would draw closer. Rather than liberating us from our roles as 'cogs' in a consumerist machine...'The necessity of survival in Ecotopia would likely make us slaves – both materially, and politically.'

Liberty has always been a delicate balance between freedom and order. Unfortunately, offences such as obstruction and 'anti-social behaviour' are so broadly and vaguely defined in legislation that they can be used to apply to almost any set of circumstances. In January 2011, the dismantling of the police network of agents undercover in the climate movement began, after constabularies across Britain decided to pull out their spies. The Metropolitan police have now absorbed the limited company police operation (*ACPO*). Then, of course, there is the publicity that undercover policing has given the movement: 'Would it be naïve to suggest that organisations whose essential endgame goal is to save the planet don't need to be spied upon like they're a terrorist cell?' (Orange TV blog).

Had the giant vertically integrated corporations really won out over horizontally detached individuals? Foreign investment took place in an unprecedented era of privatisation, which saw national assets, such as utilities, the electricity-generating network (CEGB), and the British Airports Authority (BAA) bought up by corporates, fulfilling their own short-term agendas.

Two courts of appeal judges overturned the conviction of the twenty environmental protesters involved with the Ratcliffe power station. Crucial evidence recorded on his watch by police spy Mark Kennedy had been withheld from the defence. Kennedy has since admitted that this was for fear they would destroy the prosecution's argument. The *IPCC* eventually had to acknowledge that the transcripts were never read by the Crown Prosecution Service. Meanwhile, Kennedy has transferred his security activities to the USA and has gone to the ground.

Under the *Criminal Procedure and Investigations Act 1996*, the police have a duty to make the CPS and the defence team aware of all evidence they have collected. The judgment is decisive as it shows how the judges did not doubt that the convictions had to be quashed, given (the failure to inform the defence of) Kennedy's role as an 'agent provocateur'. 'First, Kennedy was involved in activities which exceeded his remit, and appeared to show him as an enthusiastic supporter of the proposed occupation of the power station and, arguably, an agent provocateur.'

Kennedy was instructed by his handler at the National Public Order Intelligence Unit (*NECTU*) thus: 'UCO133 (Kennedy) will decline the offer for a solicitor. UCO133 will be engaged in driving and dropping off of activists *prior to them committing offences. UCO133 will withdraw from the vicinity of the power station* to avoid arrest and avoid becoming a witness to offences. SIO Inspector David Hutcheson will be regularly informed of the situation of UCO133 and in the event of…arrest will be immediately informed in order to liaise with the Nottinghamshire Senior management and the CPS.' The activists never even got as far as the power station as they were arrested at Sneinton School the night before.

'In two separate reports submitted by the camp to the Joint Committee on Human Rights, we highlighted that no Climate Camp protester has ever been convicted of any violent offence.'

According to the Camp press office:

'Serious issues, both moral and legal, are raised by Kennedy's conduct over several years but we cannot allow the IPCC to conduct yet another whitewash. We need to know who in the Met knew what Kennedy was doing and when they knew it, why Kennedy was used to entrapping so many activists at Ratcliffe, most of whom were never charged and six of whom he offered to support in court, and whether his wider conduct was sanctioned. The police can't be held to a lower standard than everyone else in society. It's time they were held to account.'

As human rights lawyer Michael Mansfield QC pointed out, police brutality can come from a 'unit mentality', an ethos that can get out of control. The tough approach by police and judges was having the expected effect – discouraging protest.

In January 2011, around 50 activists attempted to blockade Scotland Yard in regard to their use of undercover police infiltrating climate change groups. When Mark Kennedy realised he would immediately be disowned by the Metropolitan police, he would not speak up for his friends. He swung the other way, even alleging that he had been intimidated by them. On the plus side, an annual camp has built the movement that developed a strategy, which has become a mainstream topic of conversation. It has moved from no local co-operation (at Drax) to extensive public participation – Heathrow, Kingsnorth.

Despite this, however, a separate Independent Police Complaints Commission (IPCC) investigation had been 'largely positive' about the Kingsnorth police operation.

'First, the matters of serious public concern which led to the establishment of a public inquiry ongoing from 2016 have caused significant harm to police and will continue to do so unless the concern is allayed and public confidence is restored. That is the whole point of the Inquiry. As with the balance between confidentiality and the openness required to conduct an effective investigation into the Terms of Reference, so too with the balance between harm to policing caused by open investigation and...the context has been set by the Ministerial decision to hold a public inquiry' (Teresa May). 'The police bodies are simply wrong to suggest that erring on the side of restriction is the cautious, least-harmful, safe option. It is not. *The most fundamental risk of harm to policing lies in the Inquiry failing to conduct a sufficiently open and effective investigation to restore public confidence in undercover policing.'*

Back in Westminster, moreover, there was precious little political support for green energy from the Tory party, especially onshore wind power at that time, which had been widely criticised by many rural villagers (and potential Tory voters). In 2015, Tim Fallon announced he would 'pull the plug' on all support for new on-shore wind farms, claiming: '…we have enough already built or planned, and there is no requirement for any more…' and lamenting that we were stuck with the ones we have already got. Meanwhile, offshore wind is expanding rapidly and is no longer as expensive an option as it once was. In fact, wind power is now supplying an average of 20% of our electricity on a breezy day. We are the windiest country in Europe. Blustery weather in December 2019 helped UK wind farms generate almost 45% of the UK's electricity on a Sunday, setting a record of more than 16GW.

There had been parliamentary cross-party support for the sit-in at the Vestas wind turbine factory, though not enough to save it. 'Workers need…to carry out a feasibility study to install wind turbines and solar panels in the workplace. This has already happened in many workplaces, such as Tilbury Docks, the BBC, BT, the NHS, numerous universities and in warehouses. Renewable energy means the workplace can have its own power source, provide jobs, probably save money in the long run and reduce the organisation's carbon footprint. Reps in fossil fuel firms should fight for their employer to convert to lower-carbon alternatives and to cut their carbon footprint. Union reps in EDF, Western Power

Distribution and Sellafield have already made a start in this direction.'

We have also been limited in Britain by other forms of eco-tokenism. As a specifier, I was reminded how few UK produced eco-building products there were to choose from at that time, for example, triple-glazing (one supplier) and bio-mass boilers (none). So these items have had to be imported from Sweden and Slovenia respectively when they could have been made in this country. The Green party and others have long pleaded with the government to create the green jobs that would provide the required products; so far it seems to have fallen on death ears. The Green Investment Bank finally set up to go was now being sold off!

The campers, it was generally agreed, failed to reach out beyond their core liberal and middle-class audience to wider worker support. A camp blogger, "Kingoliver" wrote: 'The difficulty as I see it is that there are so many groups, so many actions, so much detail and too many "facts" people. Normal people and that is who we are talking about, need something to get them hooked. This is now being taken up by groups like the *Jobs Caravan* of the *Campaign* against Climate Change – partnership with the unions rather than business. Another camper wrote, "One cannot blame the core group – you can only do what you can do."'

He continued, 'There needs to be a bit more of "we can do this" and "we can do that" rather than "no this" and "no that", then we might get somewhere with attracting people from wider society.'

'The Climate Camp movement has to be applauded for the previously unimaginable levels of prominence that it has brought to the grassroots movement against environmental destruction, (in) the world of total media saturation and control with "reasons", "causes" and "solutions" inserted for each unfolding, dramatic episode of a soap opera. All over the place, from the popular culture to the propaganda system, there is constant pressure to make people feel that they are helpless, that the only role they can have is to ratify decisions and to consume.'–Noam Chomsky.

There is a different dynamic growing up around information: 'information as a social good, free at the point of use, incapable of being owned or exploited or priced. Sitting alongside the world of monopolised information and surveillance created by corporations and governments, to build a framework to understand the dynamics of an economy based on abundant, socially-held information,' according to Robert Peston.

'But it was actually imagined by one 19th-century economist in the era of the telegraph and the steam engine— Karl Marx.' One blogger put it thus:

'We are young, many of us, and have lived little; some of us are older and have forgotten. But these memories are ours, *not theirs,* and it is up to us to recover them.'

Half-memories will not do if we are to succeed. So, remember: the state is not 'us', any more than is the market; rather, the state—all states, in this modern global capitalist economy—are above all bound to serve the interests of the market; for, without maintaining a good environment for 'capital accumulation' any modern economy would soon collapse. That means the state acts in the interests of the market, and, on pain of collapse, cannot act otherwise. The state, we might say, acts in the interests of capital...'Our primary tactic at present is to throw ourselves into police custody in order to make the middle pages of the liberal press.'

One blogger wrote: 'Ultimately the "we, or us" appealed to by Monbiot and his ilk, their wilful Icarus who now has to grow up and learn to be responsible, does not exist. Monbiot will admit this, and talk about capitalism as a distorting force that must be constrained...he will talk about how it is the rich who cause climate change, and so the rich who must take the burden. But the state is not "us" any more than the "market" is.'

The media attention that brought the Climate Camp into the mainstream was replaced by mindless rage. Mainstreaming made the camp popular with liberals and the middle-classes. Niche never implies outreach. There was an element of street theatre. *Identities and rituals had become huge obstacles to change.*

To me, it was clear in hindsight that there may have been deliberate manipulation of consensus. The clever psychology of the Delphi method was that it let activists feel they owned their participation. I was surprised I had missed that, after attending most of the meetings to set up the camp! It may have been accidental at camp No 2, at Heathrow; due to a breakdown in communication between facilitators. A Camp organising meeting had agreed the month prior to the camp to occupy BAA head office, but then at the public meeting had again been thrown open to a full consensus decision. It was, however, repeated a second time. This was, I believe, because of a 'block' by some of those present. It was noticed by other bloggers. Was it merely the inexperience of new team facilitators? I am still unsure.

Consensus decision making was already showing the strain. By 2010, that antipathy led to a leadership crisis. One camper commented about the old guard: 'They were completely burned out'. A recurring complaint they had was that they weren't appreciated for their skills.' I had already left for personal reasons.

Questionable decisions had occurred, outside the *Delphi* consensus. The *Daily Mail* had been quick to point out one hypocrisy. I quote: 'A decision by a climate-change group to fly leading activists 12,000 miles to a conference (in South America) threatens to tear the movement apart. The "leadership" of Climate Camp—which is opposed to flying and airport expansion—has been accused of hypocrisy after they sent two members on a £1,200 round-trip flight to Bolivia.' This event was the Peoples World conference on climate change in Cochabamba, (an event hosted by the late Hugo Chavez).

The dilemma of a full-on consensus decision-making model: there is no steering wheel. Direct action can only stay alive through constant innovation of tactics. The state had been able to anticipate camp tactics. The old guard was unable to adapt. Consensus had achieved all it could, but it had failed to evolve in time; it was ripe for manipulation.

The obvious conclusion: if 'zero carbon' is the problem, then 'zero-carbon' is the solution. The problem with this approach is it is not grassroots, too academic, too theoretical for general support. When a thought process like abstraction (*zero carbon*) is utilised, rather than personal experience, it creates a problem.

Clare Saunders from Southampton University wrote: 'The Camp seems to have (had) two key goals – to tackle climate change and be anti-capitalist. Surely progress on one of those goals is better than no progress at all?'

'Nobody knows the precise dynamics of what actions will change the world, but we do know that any social movement will fail to head off catastrophic climate change *if it sticks solely to the politics of climate change.* With food riots on three continents and spiralling energy costs worldwide, changes in the weather are taking a back seat to basic questions of people getting the food and energy they want. These crises are signposts to the defining issues of international solidarity and justice in the 21st century: how does humanity allocate finite resources globally? The problem is inequality: scientist Jared Diamond has calculated that the average amount of food, energy, metal and plastic consumption by an individual in Western Europe and the United States is approximately thirty-two times that of an average individual of the rest of the planet.'

'To do this will require the large-scale harvesting of the planet's ambient energy: sunlight, wind, and waver power. This means vast new conglomerations of human industry are going to appear in places where this energy is most abundant. Unfortunately, these places coincide with some of the world's wildest, most beautiful and most untouched landscapes. These are the sort of places which environmentalism came into being to protect.' This is the business-as-usual approach. We need something more convincing than compulsory corporate social responsibility, and we don't want any more oil-company subsidised community centres (as highlighted by the fate of the *Tipping Point*, as we saw in Chapter 17). So does it all come back to inequality?

The late American environmentalist Lester R. Brown was a leading proponent of a market-led solution. He wrote: 'To win, we must embark on a radical change of direction with a wartime sense of urgency.' Brown's plan had four interconnecting strands: climate stabilisation, population stabilisation, poverty eradication and ecosystem repair. For the cost of $190 billion per year, Brown suggested, this could be drawn down from global defence budgets, which are six times greater. In the UK, substantial subsidies such as the *Renewable Heat Incentive* were introduced.

'To stabilise the climate, he recommended reducing global CO_2 emissions by 80 percent by 2020–40 percent by ending deforestation, planting trees and changing farming practices. Redirecting taxes from employment to environmental damage (ideally with a tax levied on fossil fuel producing companies) would wind down the use of hydrocarbon fuels and give incentives for efficiency and renewable energy. Unless the climate risk is factored into the market, exploration will continue. We haven't time to wait for the UN, he argues: individual nations must go ahead and take action, regardless.' Of course, they are now, since the Paris Accord.

Brown (writing before the banking crisis of 2007), had believed the world could economically grow its way out of this problem. Did he see growth as the solution – a very American viewpoint? As a libertarian, he had no time for personal carbon credits or lifestyle/behaviour change; but he did acknowledge the role of vegetarianism.

According to Paul Mobbs:

'The clear way out of the climate crisis we face is to develop renewable sources of energy to build a low, ultimately zero, carbon economy as fast as possible. There is no place here for the exploitation of any new fossil fuels and especially those that carry a high intrinsic risk of a variety of damaging environmental impacts, like shale gas. This is a critical decision for the UK and for the world, *are we going to build a zero-carbon economy? We need to avert climate catastrophe, as fast as possible – or will we endlessly defer that goal as we exploit every last drop of every new source of fossil fuel we can find*, until it is too late, and we are facing disasters a hundred times worse than, for instance, the one we are seeing now in Somalia.' The nuclear debate is such a red herring because unless we come up with a waste disposal strategy, we are going to irradiate ourselves at some point in the future.

Climate campers had promoted 'bottom up' organisations but failed to communicate their ideas to the wider world. Some of their ideas had business origins – The concept of 'buddies' is widely used by, amongst others, Nandos, Walmart and Asda. So it was not some fatalistic outlook of dark green ecology, the people who say you can have a nice life by hanging out with the right people. The issue was one where there was no immediate effect on many individuals, but the knowledge that it could be a long-term threat; a chronic situation. Their occupation of physical space in which to host an experimental shared community continues to inspire.

I never really resolved the conundrum either; but I continued to practice as a designer, specialising in low carbon building. Antagonism to the outside and solidarity may create a solid basis for an organisation; but whereas the police had evolved new tactics; the campers hadn't. The initial impetus in the camp was radical and influenced government policy, but it became the product of mutual weakness and isolation. In Edinburgh, it had run its course.

Radicals are not outside society, they can be seen as the cutting edge force challenging the authority of the prevailing order to innovate the change. They do, however, require credibility and public support. The different police strategies adopted every year, by contrast, proved successful in containing the movement. One blogger wrote: 'we contend that the shying away from developing an explicit critique in favour of simply movement building has been one of these issues that have brought the Camp to its current impasse.'

'As much as we would like, we cannot allow the revolution to happen by building bigger and better Climate Camp's or organising more extreme actions.' This is a lesson that the Extinction Rebellion would do well to comprehend. Hopefully, Coronavirus is now focusing on the greater belief that countering climate change is achievable. For example, infectious disease modellers are now guiding public policy. When will the climate modellers be allowed to guide environmental policy?

Goldman writes:

'The crux of the matter is the contradiction of wishing to "protect" people from themselves. It is the antithesis of humanism. Consider, for example, a form of feminism or a racial equality movement that made the claim that women or black people needed "protection". They would be regarded as paternalistic, and probably chauvinist.' Black Lives Matter?

The fact that the young are realising what they will have to live with is probably our last best chance to attempt to reverse the direction we are heading, so all us mature people who know what is going on, really desperately need to support them and to do absolutely all we can to help them in their desperate battle. The writing's on the wall.

'We must not think that these efforts are not going to change the world. They benefit society, often unbeknown to us, for they call forth a goodness which, albeit unseen, inevitably tends to spread. Furthermore, such actions can restore our sense of self-esteem: they can enable us to live more fully and to feel that life on earth is worthwhile.'

Appendix One

Chronology of Climate Camps

Name	Attendance	Arrests	Location	Date
Drax Power Stn	600	38	N. Yorkshire, UK	August 2006
Heathrow Airport	1500	58	London, UK	August 2007
Kooragang Island	1500	26	Newcastle, NSW, Australia	July 2008
Kingsnorth Power Stn	2000	1	Maidstone, Kent, England	August 2008
Coal caravan Cycle	60	0	Between Midlands en route to Kent	April 2008
Hold-up Drax coaltrain	(29 arrests)	29	Yorkshire, UK	June 2008

Moorburg power Stn	800	?	Hamburg, Germany	August 2008
Climate 'camp' in the city	5000 (day only)	0	City of London, UK	May 2009
Blackheath	300	11	Greater London, UK	August 2009
Mainshill Wood	50	20	Ayrshire, Scotland	August 2009
Ffos-y-Fran open-cast mine	18	18	S. Wales	August 2009
Antwerp Bulk terminal	400	?	Liege, Belgium	August 2009
Nantes Airport	2000	?	Nantes, France	August 2009
West Offaly Power Station	No information	?	Shannonbridge, Eire	2009
Various 6 no.	No information	2	Edmonton, Canada	September 2009
Proposed Swoop Ratcliffe on Soar	1000	114	Nottingham, England	October 2009
Camp Aotearoa	N/A	?	Wellington, N. Zealand	December 2009
RBS Edinburgh	500	8	Edinburgh, Scotland	August 2010

Liege airport	No information	?	Belgium	August 2010
Co. Tyrone	Not known	?	Co. Tyrone, N. Ireland	01/08/10
En Seine Mare	No information	?	France	August 2010
Shell drill Blockade of Met	N/a No information	?	Skåne, Sweden London, UK	August 2010 January 2011
RWE, lignite mine	800	?	Cologne, Germany	August 2015